Beautiful Crocheted Sweaters

by Patricia Bevans

Meredith® Press

New York

For Meredith® Press:

Vice President, Editorial Director: *Elizabeth P. Rice*
Editorial Project Manager: *Barbara S. Machtiger*
Editorial Assistant: *Valerie Martone*
Production Manager: *Bill Rose*
Designer: *Diane Wagner*
Photography: *Robert Gattullo*
Painted Backgrounds: *Joy Nagy, NYC*

Dear Crocheter:

Welcome to the creative world of *Beautiful Crocheted Sweaters*. Whether you're just a beginner or an experienced hand with the crochet hook, you'll love this collection of more than 35 soft and cozy sweaters for work, play, and special occasions. Choose from vests and pullovers, jackets and cardigans, turtle-, V-, bateau-, and crew-neck styles in a wardrobe of fashionable patterns, colors, and textures.

   The striking color photographs of each project and the precise step-by-step instructions are hallmarks of Meredith Press craft books. Look for others in your Better Homes and Gardens Crafts Club catalog.

   Meanwhile, enjoy browsing through *Beautiful Crocheted Sweaters* and selecting your favorite sweater projects. They work up so quickly, you'll find yourself returning to this book again and again.

Cordially,

Barbara Machtiger

Barbara S. Machtiger
Editorial Project Manager
Meredith® Press

Distributed by Meredith Corporation. Des Moines, Iowa
ISBN: 0-696-02356-3
Library of Congress Catalog Card Number: 90−064241
Printed in the United States of America
10 9 8 7 6 5 4 3 2 1

Contents

Combination Stitch Patterns

Tunisian Crochet

Appliqué

Crochet Stitches and Techniques

Index

Yarn Suppliers

Introduction

This book includes projects for all skill levels; for those who already love to crochet and for those who are just learning.

The projects use simple stitches, combined and arranged into quickly-established patterns. A range of beautiful possibilities is covered, with techniques that include texture and color work, openwork, appliqué, and—for the adventurous—Tunisian crochet.

Complete instructions are included for each sweater. Additional information helpful for completing the projects is included in the illustrated reference section entitled "Crochet Stitches and Techniques."

There are pullovers, cardigans, turtlenecks, and jackets, styled for everyday wear and for special occasions; for breezy summer nights and for blustery winter days; to flatter both the slim and the fuller, more mature figure.

All of the projects, easily workable in handsome, practical, and affordable yarns, are designed to create colorful, comfortable fashions you'll wear everywhere your busy life takes you.

Crochet is versatile and beautiful; but more importantly, crochet is FUN! So, enjoy! Make yourself an attractive new wardrobe, and have a wonderful time doing it!

—Patricia Bevans

Getting Started

Tools and Materials

To begin, in addition to crochet hooks and yarn, you'll need:

A small ruler for measuring gauge;

A tape measure for measuring the work;

A pair of scissors for cutting the yarn;

Stainless steel pins to join sections for seaming;

A blunt-ended, small-eyed needle (such as a tapestry needle) for sewing the garment together.

HOOKS

Plastic and aluminum crochet hooks are available in sizes 1/B to 10½/K, with B being the smallest and K the largest. The hooks are approximately 5″ long and have a slight contour at the hook end.

Afghan hooks are used for Tunisian (or afghan) crochet. They are number and letter sized like conventional crochet hooks, but they are longer (10″, 14″, and 22″ flexible), of a uniform thickness, and have a knob at the end. Afghan hooks resemble knitting needles more than crochet hooks because, like knitting needles, they must hold all the stitches in a row.

Smaller hooks are appropriate for lighter weight yarns, larger hooks for heavier weight yarns.

Hook sizes are specified for each pattern. Since stitch tension varies among crocheters (some work loosely, others tightly), the hook size specified should be used as a guide only. The hook size that gives **you** the gauge specified in the pattern should be used.

A U.S. to English and Continental hook size conversion chart is included for convenience.

YARN

Yarn is categorized by fiber content, by weight, and by texture.

There are natural fibers such as wool and cotton, and man-made fibers such as acrylic and nylon. The term blend is used when several types of fiber are combined in the same yarn.

Natural fibers are thought to be softer and more durable than man-made fibers, but they are often more expensive and require more care. Man-made fibers are constantly being improved, and many are not only soft and durable but have the added advantage of being reasonably priced and easy to care for. Blends of natural and man-made fibers can have the advantages of both. Information on fiber content and care requirements is included on the yarn label.

The weight of a yarn refers to the thickness to which a fiber is spun. The thickness of a yarn determines the gauge (or number of stitches per inch) to which it can be worked. Sport, worsted, and chunky are common weights. Weight information is often provided on the label in the form of a recommended knitting gauge. Sport weight yarn has a recommended gauge of 5½ to 6 stitches per inch; worsted weight a recommended gauge of 4 to 5 stitches per inch, and chunky weight a recommended gauge of less than 4 stitches per inch. Crocheters can use recommended knitting gauge information to determine the weight of the yarn, but should not expect to get the same number of stitches per inch. Generally, crochet has fewer stitches per inch than knitting.

The texture of a yarn influences the look of the finished garment. It can be smooth, brushed, crinkled, or

CROCHET HOOKS (ALUMINUM OR PLASTIC)										
U.S.	1/B	2/C	3/D	4/E	5/F	6/G	8/H	9/I	10/J	10½/K
English	12	11	10	9	8	7	6	5	4	2
Continental—mm	2.25	2.75	3.25	3.5	3.75	4.25	5	5.5	6	6.5

bumpy. Smooth yarns emphasize the stitch most clearly, brushed yarns soften it, and crinkled or bumpy yarns obscure it.

The yarns specified in the instructions should be used to duplicate the projects in this book. However, an attractive, similar garment can be made with another yarn if some simple guidelines are followed. Always substitute a yarn with the same fiber content, weight, and texture as the one specified. Be **sure** to make a test swatch and adjust the hook size until the gauge specified in the pattern is obtained.

Yarn is sold in balls or skeins. The weight in ounces and/or grams (3½ ounces equals 100 grams; 1¾ ounces equals 50 grams) and the yardage per ball are stated on the label. Yardage is the more significant measurement, and this can vary widely from one yarn to another. When making substitutions, determine your quantity requirements by yardage so that you'll be sure to have enough yarn to complete the project.

When you are starting, always buy enough yarn to complete the project. Yarn is dyed in lots, which are indicated by a number on the label. There can be subtle variations in shade between different dye lots, which will show on a finished garment. Be sure to purchase all your balls of yarn from the same dye lot.

Easily obtainable, reasonably priced sport, worsted, and chunky weight yarns in a variety of fibers and blends were used for the projects in the book.

Understanding Crochet Patterns

Crochet patterns use standard abbreviations. A list of these abbreviations follows.

Crochet Abbreviations

bpdc	back post double crochet
ch(s)	chain(s)
ch sp	chain space
dc	double crochet
dec	decrease
fpdc	front post double crochet
hdc	half double crochet
inc	increase
k	Tunisian crochet knit stitch
lp(s)	loop(s)
MC	main color
oz	ounces
p	Tunisian crochet purl stitch
rnd	round
sc	single crochet
sk	skip
sl st	slip stitch
sp	space
st(s)	stitch(es)
tog	together
tr	triple crochet
yd	yards
yo	wrap yarn over hook
"	inches
*	repeat instructions between asterisks across or as many times as directed
( )	repeat instructions within parentheses as many times as directed

Sunrise Jacket, page 114

The sweaters in this book are sized Small, Medium, and Large. Figures for size Small appear first. Changes for sizes Medium and Large appear in parentheses ( ). When only one figure appears, it applies to all sizes.

The patterns have been graded according to the degree of skill required to complete them. If you've never crocheted before, don't despair. Refer to the instructional entitled "Crochet Stitches and Techniques" for additional information and help. With a little practice you'll soon be comfortable enough with the basics to start a beginner sweater. Remember that even the most proficient crocheters started out as beginners!

Gauge

Gauge is the term used to indicate the number of stitches and rows per inch of fabric. Working to the gauge stated in a pattern is essential for proper fit. To test the gauge, work at least a 4″ × 4″ swatch. Dividing the number of stitches by the measurement of the swatch (in inches) gives the gauge per inch. If you have **more** stitches per inch than the pattern specifies, try a larger hook; if you have **fewer** stitches try a smaller hook. Keep adjusting the hook size until you obtain the specified gauge. Even a small difference in gauge can result in a garment that does not fit properly. For example, a pattern might specify a gauge of 4 stitches per inch for a garment with a finished bust measurement of 38″. If the pattern is worked at a gauge of 4½ stitches per inch, the garment will have a finished bust measurement of 34″—a difference of 4 inches. If the same pattern were worked at a gauge of 3½ stitches per inch, the finished bust measurement would be 43″. Either would probably be unacceptable.

Check the measurement of the garment piece as you go to be sure that you are keeping to gauge. Make horizontal measurements from edge to edge, being sure that the tape measure runs straight across and is not tilted at an angle. Make vertical measurements from top to bottom, again being sure that the tape measure is not tilted at an angle.

Size

The garments in this book are sized Small, Medium and Large. Approximate finished bust, back length, and sleeve inseam measurements are provided for each size.

The width of the finished garment must include the measurement of the body bust **plus** some additional fabric, called "ease," for comfort and to permit movement. An ease of less than 4″ is considered a snug fit, 4″–6″ is a comfortable fit, and more than 6″ would be a roomy fit. The garments in this book have been designed for a comfortable to roomy fit. Size Small is intended for a body bust of 32″–34″; Medium for a body bust of 36″–38″, and Large for a body bust of 40″–42″.

Block Pattern Pullover, page 51

THE SWEATERS

Single Crochet Patterns

Rick-rack Pullover
BEGINNER

*Country-fresh and colorful rick-rack stripes
brighten this casual pullover worked in
simple stitches with a minimum of shaping.*

SIZE
Small (Medium, Large)
Finished bust: 38" (42", 46")
Back length: 22" (22½", 23")
Sleeve inseam: 6" (6½", 7")

MATERIALS
Phildar Leader (worsted weight acrylic), 3½ oz/216
   yd balls: 5 (5, 6) balls Blue (MC); 1 ball each Red
   (A), Turquoise (B), and Yellow (C)
Sizes H and J crochet hooks (or size for gauge)

GAUGE
18 sts = 4"; 18 rows = 4" (in pattern st)
Check gauge to assure proper fit.

SEE
Changing Color/End of Row, Increasing, Reverse
Slip Stitch, and Working with Chain Spaces/In

NOTE
For stitch counts, include each sc **and** each ch 1 sp

FRONT
With MC and larger hook, ch 86 (96, 104).

Border: Row 1: Sc in 2nd ch from hook and each ch
across—85 (95, 103) sts.

Row 2: Ch 1, turn, sc in first st, *ch 1, sk next st, sc
in next st*, repeat * to * across.

Row 3: Ch 1, turn, sc in first st, sc in first ch 1 sp,
ch 1, sk next st, sc in next ch 1 sp, repeat * to *
across, ending with sc in last st.

Row 4: With A, ch 1, turn, sc in first st, *ch 1, sk
next st, sc in next ch 1 sp*, repeat * to * across, ending
with sc in last st (rather than ch 1 sp).

Row 5: With A, repeat Row 3.

Stripe Pattern: Work 2 rows of each color in the following sequence: *MC, B, MC, C, MC, B, MC, A*.
Starting stripe pattern next row (repeat * to * 1 time
only), repeat Rows 4 and 3, ending with Row 3 (**border
ends**).

Body: With MC only, repeat Rows 4 and 3, ending
with Row 3, until piece measures 14" from beginning;
end.

Armhole Shaping: Sk first 10 sts, rejoin yarn and work
Row 4 across next 65 (75, 83) sts; leave remaining
stitches unworked.

Working even on 65 (75, 83) sts, repeat Rows 3 and
4, ending with Row 3, until piece measures 18" (18½",
19") from beginning.

Neck Shaping: Work Row 4 across first 19 (23, 27)
sts; leave remaining sts unworked.

Working even on 19 (23, 27) sts, repeat Rows 3 and
4 until piece measures 22" (22½", 23") from
beginning.

Leaving center 27 (29, 29) sts free, shape opposite side of neck edge to correspond.

BACK

Work as for front through armhole shaping.

Working even on 65 (75, 83) sts, repeat Rows 3 and 4, ending with Row 3, until piece measures 20" (20½", 21") from beginning.

Shape neckline as for front.

SLEEVES (make two)

With MC and larger hook, ch 62 (66, 70).

Border: **Row 1:** Sc in 2nd ch from hook and each ch across—61 (65, 69) sts.

Row 2: Ch 1, turn, sc in first st, *ch 1, sk next st, sc in next st*, repeat * to * across.

Row 3: Ch 1, turn, sc in first st, sc in first ch 1 sp, *ch 1, sk next st, sc in next ch 1 sp*, repeat * to * across, ending with sc in last st.

Row 4: With A, ch 1, turn, sc in first st, *ch 1, sk next st, sc in next ch 1 sp*, repeat * to * across, ending with sc in last st (rather than ch 1 sp).

Row 5: With A, ch 1, turn, sc in first st, ch 1, sc in first ch 1 sp (**inc made**), *ch 1, sk next st, sc in next ch 1 sp*, repeat * to * across, ending with ch 1, sc in last st (**inc made**)—63 (67, 71) sts.

Starting stripe pattern of front next row, repeat Rows 3, 4, and 5, ending with Row 3 (**border ends**).

With MC, repeat Rows 4 and 5 one time more—75 (79, 83) sts.

Working even on 75 (79, 83) sts, with MC only, repeat Rows 3 and 4 until piece measures 8" (8½", 9") from beginning.

FINISHING

With right sides facing, sew front to back at shoulder seams, sleeves to sleeve openings, sleeve and side seams.

Edging: With right side facing, MC and smaller hook, start at center back and work 1 rnd sc around neck opening; join with sl st to first sc. Ch 1, don't turn, work 1 rnd reverse sl st into previous rnd; join with sl st to first reverse sl st; end.

Finish bottom and sleeve edges in same manner.

Secure and trim loose ends.

Mosaic Pullover

BEGINNER

Rich jewel tones offset a dramatic black background in this Byzantine-inspired mosaic sweater.

SIZE
Small (Medium, Large)
Finished bust: 38" (42", 46")
Back length: 21½" (22", 22½")

MATERIALS
Reynolds Reynelle Deluxe (worsted weight acrylic), 3½ oz/240 yd balls: 3 balls Black (MC); 1 ball each Lilac (A), Mauve (B), and Pink (C)
Sizes H and I crochet hooks (or size for gauge)

GAUGE
18 sts = 4"; 19 rows = 4" (in pattern st)
Check gauge to assure proper fit.

SEE
Changing Color/End of Row, Decreasing/Single Crochet, Reverse Slip Stitch, Surface Slip Stitch, and Working with Chain Spaces/In

NOTE
For stitch counts, include each sc **and** each ch 1 sp

FRONT
With MC and larger hook, ch 88 (96, 104).

Row 1: Sc in 2nd ch from hook and each ch across—87 (95, 103) sts.

Row 2: With MC, ch 1, turn, sc in first st, sc in next st, *ch 1, sk next st, sc in next st*, repeat * to * across, ending with sc in last st.

Row 3: With A, ch 1, turn, sc in first st, *ch 1, sk next st, sc in next ch 1 sp*, repeat * to * across, ending with sc in last st (rather than ch 1 sp).

Row 4: With A, ch 1, turn, sc in first st, sc in first ch 1 sp, *ch 1, sk next st, sc in next ch 1 sp*, repeat * to * across, ending with sc in last st.

Stripe Pattern: *1 row MC, 2 rows B, 1 row MC, 2 rows C, 1 row MC, 2 rows A*. Starting stripe pattern next row (repeat * to * throughout), repeat Rows 3 and 4, ending with Row 3, until piece measures 13½" from beginning; end.

Armhole Shaping: Sk first 10 sts, **keeping to stripe pattern, as established,** rejoin yarn and work Row 4 across next 67 (75, 83) sts; leave remaining sts unworked.

Next (Dec) Row: Ch 1, turn, sk first st **(dec made)**, sc in next st, sc in first ch 1 sp, *ch 1, sk next st, sc in next ch 1 sp*, repeat * to * across, ending with sc 2 tog over last 2 sts **(dec made)**.

Next Row: Repeat Row 3.

Next (Dec) Row: Ch 1, sk first st **(dec made)**, sc in first ch 1 sp, *ch 1, sk next st, sc in next ch 1 sp* repeat * to * across, ending with ch 1, sc 2 tog over last ch 1 sp and st **(dec made)**.

Next Row: Repeat Row 4.

Repeat the last 4 rows 2 times more.

Working even on 55 (63, 71) sts, repeat Rows 3 and 4, ending with Row 4, until piece measures 17″ from beginning.

Neck Shaping: Continuing to keep to stripe pattern, as established, work Row 3 across first 21 (25, 29) sts; leave remaining sts unworked.

Next (Dec) Row: Ch 1, turn, sk first st (**dec made**), sc in first ch 1 sp, *ch 1, sk next st, sc in next ch 1 sp*, repeat * to * across, ending with sc in last st.

Next (Dec) Row: Ch 1, turn, sc in first st, *ch 1, sk next st, sc in next ch 1 sp*, repeat * to * across, ending with ch 1, sc 2 tog over last ch 1 sp and st (**dec made**).

Repeat the last 2 rows 1 time more.

Working even on 17 (21, 25) sts, repeat Row 4, then Rows 3 and 4 until piece measures 21½″ (22″, 22½″) from beginning.

Leaving center 13 sts free, shape opposite side of neck edge to correspond.

BACK

With MC only, work as for front through armhole shaping.

Working even on 55 (63, 71 sts), repeat Rows 3 and 4, ending with Row 4, until piece measures 19½″ (20″, 20½″) from beginning.

Shape neckline as for front.

FINISHING

With right sides facing, sew front to back at shoulder and side seams.

Edging: With right side facing, MC and smaller hook, start at center back and work 1 rnd sc around neck opening; join with sl st to first sc. Ch 1, don't turn, work 1 rnd reverse sl st into previous rnd; join with sl st to first reverse sl st. Ch 1, don't turn, working **below** previous rnd, work 1 rnd surface sl st around posts of first edging rnd; join with sl st to first surface sl st. Repeat the last rnd 1 time more; end.

Finish bottom and armhole edges in same manner.

Secure and trim loose ends.

Chanel-style Suit

BEGINNER

A beginner's project that's sure to impress.
The timeless styling of this two-piece ensemble makes it
a classic addition to any wardrobe.

SIZE
Small (Medium, Large)
Jacket:
Finished bust: 38" (42", 46")
Back length: 21½" (22", 22½")
Sleeve inseam: 17½" (18", 18½")
Skirt:
Finished hip: 40" (44", 48")
Length: 25" (25½", 26")

MATERIALS
Unger Fluffy (brushed, worsted weight acrylic),
   1¾ oz/156 yd balls: 7 (8, 9) balls White (A); 7
   (8, 9) balls Medium Aqua (B)
Sizes I and J crochet hooks (or size for gauge)
1 (1, 1½) yds ¾" waistband elastic; large safety pin;
   sewing needle; sewing thread

GAUGE
19 sts = 4"; 18 rows = 4" (in pattern st)
Check gauge to assure proper fit.

SEE
Decreasing/Single Crochet, Increasing, Reverse Slip
Stitch, and Surface Slip Stitch

NOTE
For stitch counts, include each sc **and** each ch 1 sp

Jacket

FRONT SIDE ONE

With A and larger hook, ch 46 (50, 56).

Row 1: Sc in 2nd ch from hook and each ch across—
45 (49, 55) sts.

Row 2: Ch 1, turn, sc in first st, *ch 1, sk next st, sc
in next st*, repeat * to * across.

Row 3: Ch 1, turn, sc in first st, sc in first ch 1 sp,
ch 1, sk next st, sc in next ch 1 sp, repeat * to *
across, ending with sc in last st.

Row 4: Ch 1, turn, sc in first st, *ch 1, sk next st, sc
in next ch 1 sp*, repeat * to * across, ending with sc
in last st (rather than ch 1 sp).

Repeat Rows 3 and 4, ending with Row 4, until piece
measures 13½" from beginning.

Armhole Shaping: Work Row 3 across first 41 (45, 51)
sts; leave remaining sts unworked.

Next (Dec) Row: Ch 1, turn, sk first st **(dec made)**,
sc in next st, sc in first ch 1 sp, *ch 1, sk next st, sc
in next ch 1 sp*, repeat * to * across, ending with sc
in last st (rather than ch 1 sp).

Next Row: Work as for Row 3 across, but end with 1
sc (rather than 2).

Next (Dec) Row: Ch 1, turn, sk first st (**dec made**), sc in first ch 1 sp, *ch 1, sk next st, sc in next ch 1 sp*, repeat * to * across, ending with sc in last st (rather than ch 1 sp).

Next Row: Repeat Row 3.

Repeat the last 4 rows 1 time more.

Working even on 37 (41, 47) sts, repeat Row 4, then Rows 3 and 4, ending with Row 3, until piece measures 18½″ from beginning.

Neck Shaping: Work Row 4 across first 27 (31, 37) sts; leave remaining sts unworked.

Next (Dec) Row: Ch 1, turn, sk first st (**dec made**), sc in first ch 1 sp, *ch 1, sk next st, sc in next ch 1 sp*, repeat * to * across, ending with sc in last st.

Next Row: Work as for Row 4 across but end with 2 sc (rather than 1).

Next (Dec) Row: Ch 1, turn, sk first st (**dec made**), sc in next st, sc in first ch 1 sp, *ch 1, sk next st, sc in next ch 1 sp*, repeat * to * across, ending with sc in last st.

Next Row: Repeat Row 4.

Repeat the last 4 rows 1 time more.

Working even on 23 (27, 33) sts repeat Rows 3 and 4 until piece measures 21½″ (22″, 22½″) from beginning.

FRONT SIDE TWO

Work as for Front Side One, reversing armhole and neck shaping.

BACK

With A and larger hook, ch 92 (100, 112).

Row 1: Sc in 2nd ch from hook and each ch across—91 (99, 111) sts.

Work Rows 2–4 as for Front, but on 91 (99, 111) sts.

Repeat Rows 3 and 4, ending with Row 4, until piece measures 13½″ from beginning; end.

Armhole Shaping: Sk first 4 sts, rejoin yarn and work Row 3 across next 83 (91, 103) sts; leave remaining sts unworked.

Next (Dec) Row: Ch 1, turn, sk first st (**dec made**), sc in next st, sc in first ch 1 sp, *ch 1, sk next st, sc in next ch 1 sp*, repeat * to * across, ending with sc 2 tog over last 2 sts (**dec made**).

Next Row: Repeat Row 4.

Next (Dec) Row: Ch 1, turn, sk first st (**dec made**), sc in first ch 1 sp, *ch 1, sk next st, sc in next ch 1 sp*, repeat * to * across, ending with ch 1, sc 2 tog over last ch 1 sp and st (**dec made**).

Next Row: Repeat Row 3.

Repeat the last 4 rows 1 time more.

Working even on 75 (83, 95) sts, repeat Row 4, then Rows 3 and 4, ending with Row 3, until piece measures 20½″ (21″, 21½″) from beginning.

Neck Shaping: Work Row 4 across first 25 (29, 35) sts; leave remaining sts unworked.

Work decrease rows of front neck shaping one time only.

Next Row: Working even on 23 (27, 33) sts, repeat Row 4.

Leaving center 25 sts free, shape opposite side of neck edge to correspond.

SLEEVES (make two)

With A and larger hook, ch 44 (48, 52).

Row 1: Sc in 2nd ch from hook and each ch across—43 (47, 51) sts.

Row 2: Ch 1, turn, sc in first st, *ch 1, sk next st, sc in next st*, repeat * to * across.

Row 3: Ch 1, turn, sc in first st, sc in first ch 1 sp, *ch 1, sk next st, sc in next ch 1 sp*, repeat * to * across, ending with sc in last st.

Row 4: Ch 1, turn, 2 sc in first st (**inc made**), *ch 1, sk next st, sc in next ch 1 sp*, repeat * to * across, ending with ch 1, sk next st, 2 sc in last st (**inc made**).

Row 5: Ch 1, turn, sc in first st, *ch 1, sk next st, sc in next ch 1 sp*, repeat * to * across, ending with sc in last st (rather than ch 1 sp).

Row 6: Repeat Row 3.

Row 7: Repeat Row 5.

Row 8: Ch 1, turn, sc in first st, ch 1, sc in first ch 1 sp (**inc made**), *ch 1, sk next st, sc in next ch 1 sp*, repeat * to * across, ending with ch 1, sc in last st (**inc made**)—47 (51, 55) sts.

Rows 9–11: Repeat Rows 3 and 5, ending with Row 3.

Repeat Rows 4–11 eight times more.

Working even on 79 (83, 87) sts, repeat Rows 5 and 3, ending with Row 5, until piece measures 17½″ (18″, 18½″) from beginning; end.

Shape Cap: Sk first 4 sts, rejoin yarn and work Row 3 across next 71 (75, 79) sts; leave remaining sts unworked.

Next (Dec) Row: Ch 1, turn, sk first st (**dec made**), sc in next st, sc in first ch 1 sp, *ch 1, sk next st, sc in next ch 1 sp*, repeat * to * across, ending with sc 2 tog over last 2 sts (**dec made**).

Next Row: Repeat Row 5.

Next (Dec) Row: Ch 1, turn, sk first st (**dec made**), sc in first ch 1 sp, *ch 1, sk next st, sc in next ch 1 sp*, repeat * to * across, ending with ch 1, sc 2 tog over last ch 1 sp and st (**dec made**).

Next Row: Repeat Row 3.

Repeat the first decrease row, then Row 5, then the last decrease row—63 (67, 71) sts.

Next (Dec) Row: Ch 1, turn, sk first st (**dec made**), sc in first ch 1 sp, *ch 1, sk next st, sc in next ch 1 sp*, repeat * to * across, ending with ch 1, sc 2 tog over last ch 1 sp and st (**dec made**).

Repeat the last row until 33 sts remain.

FINISHING

With right sides facing, sew front panels to back at shoulder seams, sleeves to sleeve openings, sleeve and side seams.

Edging: With right side facing, B and smaller hook, start at side seam and work 1 rnd sc around entire garment edge (bottom, center front, and neckline), **working 3 sc at each corner;** join with sl st to first sc. Ch 1, don't turn, work 1 rnd reverse sl st into previous rnd; join with sl st to first reverse sl st. Ch 1, don't turn, working **below** previous rnd, work 1 rnd surface sl st around posts of first edging rnd; join with sl st to first sl st. Repeat the last rnd 1 time more; end.

Finish sleeve edges in same manner.

Secure and trim loose ends.

Skirt

FRONT/BACK (make two)

With B and larger hook, ch 78 (88, 98) sts.

Row 1: Sc in 2nd ch from hook and each ch across—77 (87, 97) sts.

Rows 2–4: Work as for Rows 2–4 of Jacket Front, but on 77 (87, 97) sts.

Rows 5–11: Repeat Rows 3 and 4, ending with Row 3.

Row 12: Ch 1, turn, 2 sc in first st (**inc made**), *ch 1, sk next st, sc in next ch 1 sp*, repeat * to * across, ending with ch 1, sk next st, 2 sc in last st (**inc made**).

Row 13: Repeat Row 4.

Row 14: Ch 1, turn, sc in first st, ch 1, sc in first ch 1 sp (**inc made**), *ch 1, sk next st, sc in next ch 1 sp*, repeat * to * across, ending with ch 1, sc in last st (**inc made**).

Rows 15–18: Repeat Rows 11–14—85 (95, 105) sts.

Rows 19–21: Repeat Rows 3 and 4, ending with Row 3.

Row 22: Repeat Row 12.

Row 23: Repeat Row 4.

Rows 24–25: Repeat Rows 3 and 4.

Row 26: Repeat Row 14—89 (99, 109) sts.

Rows 27–58: Repeat Rows 19–26—105 (115, 125) sts.

Rows 59–65: Repeat Rows 3 and 4, ending with Row 3.

Row 66: Repeat Row 12.

Row 67: Repeat Row 4.

Rows 68–73: Repeat Rows 3 and 4.

Row 74: Repeat Row 14—109 (119, 129) sts.

Repeat Rows 59–74 two times more, then Rows 59–66 one time.

Working even on 119 (129, 139) sts, repeat Row 4, then Rows 3 and 4 three (four, five) times (or to desired length).

FINISHING

With right sides facing, sew front to back at side seams.

Turn skirt wrong side out. Turn upper edge back 1″ to form waistband casing. Sew down with hem stitch, **leaving a 1½″ opening** for threading elastic. Cut elastic to waist measurement plus 2″. Attach safety pin to elastic end and thread through waistband casing. Using sewing needle and sewing thread, sew short ends of elastic together securely. Using yarn and hem stitch, close waistband casing.

Finish hemline by working edging rnds in same manner as for jacket.

Secure and trim loose ends.

Polka Dot Tank Top

BEGINNER

Lavender polka dots brighten a summery white tank top
to wear with a skirt, slacks, or shorts.

SIZE
Small (Medium, Large)
Finished bust: 38″ (42″, 46″)
Back length: 21″ (21½″, 22″)

MATERIALS
Brunswick Pearl (worsted weight acrylic), 1¾ oz/
   110 yd balls: 8 (9, 10) balls White (MC); 2 balls
   Lavender (CC)
Sizes H and I crochet hooks (or size for gauge)

GAUGE
17 sts = 4″; 27 rows = 4″ (in pattern st)
Check gauge to assure proper fit.

SEE
Changing Color/End of Row, Decreasing/Single
Crochet, Working with Chain Spaces/In Front of,
Reverse Slip Stitch, and Surface Slip Stitch

FRONT

With MC and larger hook, ch 82 (90, 98).

Row 1: Sc in 2nd ch from hook and each ch across—
81 (89, 97) sts.

Rows 2–3: Ch 1, turn, sc in first st and each st across.

Row 4: With CC, ch 1, turn, sc in first st, *ch 1, sk
next st, sc in next st*, repeat * to * across.

Row 5 (right side): With MC, ch 1, turn, sc in first
st, working in **front** of ch 1 previous row, sc in first
sk st of that row, *sc in next st, working in **front** of
ch 1 previous row, sc in next sk st of that row*, repeat
* to * across, ending with sc in last st.

Row 6: With CC, ch 1, turn, sc in first 2 sts, *ch 1,
sk next st, sc in next st*, repeat * to * across, ending
with sc in last st.

Row 7: With MC, ch 1, turn, sc in first 2 sts, working
in **front** of ch 1 previous row, sc in first sk st of that
row, *sc in next st, working in **front** of ch 1 previous
row, sc in next sk st of that row*, repeat * to * across,
ending with sc in last 2 sts.

Rows 8–13: Repeat Rows 4–7 one time more, then
Rows 4–5 one time.

Rows 14–15: With MC, ch 1, turn, sc in first st and
each st across.

Rows 16–17: Repeat Rows 4–5.

Rows 18–19: Repeat Rows 14–15.

Repeat Rows 4–19 four times more, then Rows 4–9
one time; end.

Armhole Shaping: Sk first 6 sts, join CC and work
Row 6 across next 69 (77, 85) sts; leave remaining sts
unworked.

Next (Dec) Row: With MC, ch 1, turn, sk first st (**dec
made**), work as for Row 5 across, ending with sc 2 tog
over last 2 sts (**dec made**).

Next Row: Repeat Row 6.

Next (Dec) Row: Repeat first decrease row.

Next Row: Repeat Row 14.

Next (Dec) Row: Decreasing 1 st each edge, repeat Row 15.

Next Row: Repeat Row 6.

Next (Dec) Row: Repeat first decrease row.

Working even on 61 (69, 77) sts, repeat Rows 18–19, then Rows 4–19 one time more.

Neck Shaping: Work Row 4 across first 19 (23, 27) sts, sc in next st; leave remaining sts unworked.

Next (Dec) Row: With MC, ch 1 turn, sk first st (**dec made**), work as for Row 5 across.

Next Row: Repeat Row 6.

Next (Dec) Row: Work as for first **Neck** decrease row, **but** end with sc in last **2** sts.

Next Row: Work as for Row 4, **but** end with sc in last 2 sts.

Repeat the last 4 rows 1 time more, then repeat first **Neck** decrease row 1 time.

Working even on 15 (19, 23) sts repeat Rows 14–19, then Rows 4–14 (17, 19).

Size Large Only: Repeat Row 19 one time more.

All Sizes: Leaving center 21 sts free, shape opposite side of neck edge to correspond.

BACK

Work as for front through Row 2.

With MC only, repeat Row 2 until piece measures 13¾″ from beginning; end.

Armhole Shaping: Sk first 6 sts, rejoin yarn and sc across next 69 (77, 85) sts; leave remaining sts unworked.

Continuing in sc, dec 1 st each edge next row and every other row 3 times.

Work even in sc on 61 (69, 77) sts until piece measures 18″ (18½″, 19″) from beginning.

Neck Shaping: Ch 1, turn, sc across first 20 (24, 28) sts; leave remaining sts unworked.

Continuing in sc, dec 1 st at neck edge next row and every other row 4 times.

Work even in sc on 15 (19, 23) sts until piece measures 21″ (21½″, 22″) from beginning.

Leaving center 21 sts free, shape opposite side of neck edge to correspond.

FINISHING

With right sides facing, sew front to back at shoulder and side seams.

Edging: With right side facing, MC and smaller hook, start at center back and work 1 rnd sc around neck opening; join with sl st to first sc. Ch 1, don't turn, work 1 rnd reverse sl st into previous rnd; join with sl st to first reverse sl st. Ch 1, don't turn, working **below** previous rnd, work 1 rnd surface sl st around posts of first edging rnd; join with sl st to first surface sl st. Repeat the last rnd 1 time more; end.

Finish bottom and armhole edges in same manner.

Secure and trim loose ends.

Polka Dot Pullover

BEGINNER

Navy blue and green flecks highlight a short-sleeved pullover that's perfect for casual dressing.

SIZE
Small (Medium, Large)
Finished bust: 38″ (42″, 47″)
Back length: 22″
Sleeve inseam: 4½″

MATERIALS
Phildar Leader (worsted weight acrylic), 3½ oz/216 yd balls: 5 (5, 6) balls White (MC); 1 ball each Navy (A) and Green (B)
Sizes H and J crochet hooks (or size for gauge)

GAUGE
18 sts = 4″; 29 rows = 5″ (in pattern st)
Check gauge to assure proper fit.

SEE
Changing Color/End of Row, Decreasing/Single Crochet, and Working with Chain Spaces/Behind

NOTE
For stitch counts, include each sc **and** each ch 1 sp

FRONT

Bottom Rib: With MC and smaller hook, ch 16.

Row 1: Sc in 2nd ch from hook and each ch across—15 sts.

Rows 2–85 (95, 105): Ch 1, turn, sc in back lp only of first st and each st across. Ch 1, work 85 (95, 105) sc evenly spaced across long edge of rib. Change to larger hook.

Body: **Rows 1–3:** Ch 1, turn, sc in first st and each st across.

Row 4: With A, ch 1, turn, sc in first st, *ch 1, sk next st, sc in next st*, repeat * to * across.

Row 5 (wrong side): With MC, ch 1, turn, sc in first st, working **behind** ch 1 of previous row, sc in first sk st of that row, *sc in next st, working **behind** ch 1 of previous row, sc in next sk st of that row*, repeat * to * across, ending with sc in last st.

Rows 6–7: With MC, repeat Row 1.

Row 8: With B, repeat Row 4.

Rows 9–11: Repeat Rows 5–7.

Repeat Rows 4–11 nine times more, then Rows 4–7.

Neck Shaping: Work Row 8 across first 31 (35, 39) sts; leave remaining sts unworked.

Next (Dec) Row: With MC, ch 1, turn, sk first st (**dec made**), working **behind** ch 1 of previous row, sc in first sk st of that row, *sc in next st, working **behind** ch 1 of previous row, sc in next sk st of that row*, repeat * to * across, ending with sc in last st.

Next Row: Repeat Row 1.

Next (Dec) Row: Ch 1, turn, sk first st (**dec made**), complete as for Row 1 across.

Next Row: Repeat Row 4.

Repeat the first decrease row, then Row 1, then the last decrease row.

Working even on 27 (31, 35) sts, repeat Rows 8–11, then Rows 4–11 one time.

Leaving center 23 (25, 27) sts free, shape opposite side of neck edge to correspond.

BACK

Work as for front through Row 11.

Repeat Rows 4–11 eleven times more.

Work Row 4 across first 29 (33, 37) sts; leave remaining sts unworked.

Repeat decrease rows of front neck shaping 1 time only.

Working even on 27 (31, 35) sts, repeat Rows 8–11.

Leaving center 27 (29, 31) sts free, shape opposite side of neck edge to correspond.

SLEEVES (make two)

Rib: With MC and smaller hook, ch 6.

Row 1: Sc in 2nd ch from hook and each ch across.

Rows 2–45 (47, 49): Ch 1, turn, sc in back lp only of first st and each st across. Ch 1, work 65 (69, 73) sc evenly spaced across long edge of rib. Change to larger hook.

Working even on 65 (69, 73) sts, work Rows 1–11 as for front.

Repeat Rows 4–11 one time more.

FINISHING

With right sides facing, sew front to back at shoulder seams. Center sleeves at shoulder seams and sew together. Sew sleeve and side seams.

Neckband: With MC and smaller hook, start at center back and work 95 (99, 103) sc evenly spaced around neck opening; join with sl st to first sc; end.

Rib: Work rib as for sleeve but for 95 (99, 103) rows. Ch 1, work 95 (99, 103) sc evenly spaced across long edge of rib.

Starting at center back, with right sides facing, sew neckband to neck opening and short edges of neckband together.

Secure and trim loose ends.

Pullover with Scallop-Striped Sleeves

BEGINNER

*The brilliant colors on the sleeves of this festive,
south-of-the-border-inspired V-neck evoke a flaming sunset.*

SIZE

Small (Medium, Large)
Finished bust: 38″ (42″, 46″)
Back length: 21½″ (22″, 22½″)
Sleeve inseam: 5″

MATERIALS

Phildar Leader (worsted weight acrylic), 3½ oz/216
 yd balls: 5 (6, 6) balls White (MC); 1 ball each
 Coral (A) and Hot Pink (B)
Sizes I and J crochet hooks (or size for gauge)

GAUGE

16 sts = 4″; 20 rows = 4″ (in pattern st)
Check gauge to assure proper fit.

SEE

Changing Color/End of Row, Decreasing/Single
Crochet, Reverse Slip Stitch, Surface Slip Stitch,
and Working with Chain Spaces/Behind

FRONT

Bottom Rib: With MC and smaller hook, ch 16.

Row 1: Sc in 2nd ch from hook and each ch across—
15 sts.

Rows 2–77 (85, 93): Ch 1, turn, sc in back lp only
of first st and each st across. Ch 1, work 77 (85, 93)
sc evenly spaced across long edge of rib. Change to
larger hook.

Body: **Row 1:** Ch 1, turn, sc in first st and each st
across. Repeat Row 1 until piece measures 13½″ from
beginning; end.

Armhole/Neck Shaping: Sk first 4 sts, rejoin yarn and
sc across next 69 (77, 85) sts; leave remaining sts
unworked.

Next (Dec) Row: Continuing in sc, dec 1 st each edge.

Next Row: Ch 1, turn, sc across first 33 (37, 41) sts;
leave remaining sts unworked.

Continuing in sc, dec 1 st each edge next row and
every other row 2 times.

Work even in sc on 27 (31, 35) sts for 1 row.

Continuing in sc, dec 1 st **at neck edge only,** next
row and every other row 10 (11, 12) times.

Work even in sc on 16 (19, 22) sts for 10 rows.

Leaving center st free, shape opposite side to
correspond.

BACK

Work as for front to armhole shaping.

Armhole Shaping: Sk first 4 sts, rejoin yarn and sc
across next 69 (77, 85) sts; leave remaining sts
unworked.

Continuing in sc, dec 1 st each edge next row and
every other row 3 times.

Work even in sc on 61 (69, 77) sts until piece measures 20½" (21", 21½") from beginning.

Neck Shaping: Ch 1, turn, sc across first 18 (21, 24) sts; leave remaining sts unworked.

Continuing in sc, dec 1 st at neck edge next row and every other row 1 time.

Work even in sc on 16 (19, 22) sts for 1 row.

Leaving center 25 (27, 29) sts free, shape opposite side of neck edge to correspond.

SLEEVES (make two)

With MC and larger hook, ch 72 (76, 80).

Row 1: Sc in 2nd ch from hook and each ch across—71 (75, 79) sts.

Rows 2–3: Ch 1, turn, sc in first st and each st across.

Row 4: With A, ch 1, turn, sc in first st, *ch 1, sk next st, sc in next st*, repeat * to * across.

Row 5 (right side): With MC, ch 1, turn, sc in first st, working **behind** ch 1 of previous row, sc in first sk st of that row, *sc in next st, working **behind** ch 1 of previous row, sc in next sk st of that row*, repeat * to * across, ending with sc in last st.

Rows 6–7: With MC, repeat Row 2.

Row 8: With B, repeat Row 4.

Rows 9–11: Repeat Rows 5–7.

Repeat Rows 4–11 two times more; end.

Shape Cap: Sk first 4 sts, join A and work Row 4 across next 63 (67, 71) sts; leave remaining sts unworked.

Next (Dec) Row: With MC, ch 1, turn, sk first st (**dec made**), working **behind** ch 1 of previous row, sc in first sk st of that row, sc in next st, *working **behind** ch 1 of previous row, sc in next sk st of that row, sc in next st*, repeat * to * across until 2 sts remain, end as follows: working **behind** ch 1 of previous row, insert hook in last sk st of that row, yo, draw up a lp, insert hook in last st, yo, draw up a lp, yo, draw through all 3 lps on hook (**dec made**).

Next Row: Repeat Row 2.

Next (Dec) Row: Decreasing 1 st each edge, repeat Row 2.

Next Row: Repeat Row 8.

Repeat the first decrease row, then Row 2, then the last decrease row—55 (59, 61) sts.

Next (Dec) Row: With A, ch 1, turn, sk first st (**dec made**), sc in first 2 sts, *ch 1, sk next st, sc in next st*, repeat * to * across, ending with sc 2 tog over last 2 sts (**dec made**).

Next (Dec) Row: With MC, ch 1, turn, sk first st (**dec made**), work as for Row 5 across, ending with sc 2 tog over last 2 sts (**dec made**).

Decreasing 1 st each edge every row, repeat Row 2 two times.

Keeping to color stripe pattern, as established, repeat the last 4 rows until 15 sts remain.

FINISHING

With right sides facing, sew front to back at shoulder seams, sleeves to sleeve openings, sleeve and side seams.

Edging: With right side facing, MC and smaller hook, start at center back and work 1 rnd sc around neck opening (**Note: Work sc 3 tog at V**); join with sl st to first sc. With B, ch 1, don't turn, work 1 rnd sc into previous rnd (**Note: Work sc 3 tog at V**); join with sl st to first sc. With B only, ch 1, don't turn, work 1 rnd reverse sl st into previous rnd; join with sl st to first reverse sl st. Ch 1, don't turn, work 1 rnd surface sl st around posts of first B edging rnd; join with sl st to first reverse sl st. Repeat the last rnd 1 time more; end.

With right side facing, MC and smaller hook, start at side seam and work 45 (49, 53) sc evenly spaced around sleeve opening. Work B edging rnds as for neckline.

Repeat on other sleeve edge.

Secure and trim loose ends.

Patterned Pullover with Collar

INTERMEDIATE

*Take the chill out of autumn with this cozy, collared sweater
just right for walking in the woods.*

SIZE

Small (Medium, Large)
Finished bust: 38″ (43″, 47″)
Back length: 22″ (22½″, 23″)
Sleeve inseam: 17½″ (18″, 18½″)

MATERIALS

Pingouin Le Yarn 3 (worsted weight acrylic, wool,
and polypropylene blend), 3½ oz/200 yd balls: 6
(6, 7) balls Copper (MC); 1 ball Cream (CC)
Sizes J and K crochet hooks (or size for gauge)

GAUGE

7 sts = 2″; 9 rows = 2″ (in pattern st)
Check gauge to assure proper fit.

SEE

Changing Color/End of Row, Decreasing/Single
Crochet, Increasing, and Working with Chain
Spaces/Behind

NOTE

For stitch counts, include each sc **and** each ch 1 sp

FRONT SIDE ONE

Bottom Rib: With MC and smaller hook, ch 16.

Row 1: Sc in 2nd ch from hook and each ch across—
15 sts.

Rows 2–67 (75, 83): Ch 1, turn, sc in back lp only
of first st and each st across. Ch 1, work 67 (75, 83)
sc evenly spaced across long edge of rib. Change to
larger hook.

Body: **Rows 1–2:** With CC, ch 1, turn, sc in first st
and each st across.

Row 3: With MC, ch 1, turn, sc in first st, *ch 1, sk
next st, sc in next st*, repeat * to * across.

Row 4 (right side): With CC, ch 1, turn, sc in first
st, working **behind** ch 1 of previous row, sc in first sk
st of that row, *sc in next st, working **behind** ch 1 of
previous row, sc in next sk st of that row*, repeat * to
* across, ending with sc in last st.

Row 5: With MC, ch 1, turn, sc in first 2 sts, *ch 1,
sk next st, sc in next st*, repeat * to * across, ending
with sc in last st.

Row 6: With CC, ch 1, turn, sc in first 2 sts, working
behind ch 1 of previous row, sc in first sk st of that
row, *sc in next st, working **behind** ch 1 of previous
row, sc in next sk st of that row*, repeat * to * across,
ending with sc in last 2 sts.

Row 7: With CC, repeat Row 1.

Rows 8–12: With MC, repeat Row 1.

Repeat Rows 1–12 three times more; end.

Armhole Shaping: Sk first 3 sts, join CC and work
Row 1 across next 61 (69, 77) sts; leave remaining sts
unworked.

Next (Dec) Row: Decreasing 1 st each edge, repeat Row 2.

Next Row: Repeat Row 3.

Next (Dec) Row: With CC, ch 1, turn, sk first st (**dec made**), working **behind** ch 1 of previous row, sc in first sk st of that row, sc in next st, *working **behind** ch 1 of previous row, sc in next sk st of that row, sc in next st*, repeat * to * across, until 2 sts remain, end as follows: working **behind** ch 1 of previous row, insert hook in last sk st of that row, yo, draw up a lp, insert hook in last st, yo, draw up a lp, yo, draw through all 3 lps on hook (**dec made**).

Repeat the last 2 rows 1 time more.

Working even on 55 (63, 71) sts, repeat Rows 7–12, then Rows 1–12.

Neck Shaping: Work Row 1 across first 18 (22, 26) sts; leave remaining sts unworked.

Next (Dec) Row: Ch 1, sk first st (**dec made**), complete as for Row 2 across.

Next Row: Repeat Row 3.

Next (Dec) Row: With CC, ch 1, turn, sk first st (**dec made**), working **behind** ch 1 of previous row, sc in first sk st of that row, *sc in next st, working **behind** ch 1 of previous row, sc in next sk st of that row*, repeat * to * across, ending with sc in last st.

Next Row: Work as for Row 5 across **but** end with 1 sc (rather than 2).

Next (Dec) Row: Work as for first neck decrease row **but** end with 2 sc (rather than 1).

Working even on 15 (19, 23) sts, repeat Rows 7–12.

Size Medium Only: With MC, repeat Row 1 two times.

Size Large Only: Repeat Rows 1–4 one time.

All Sizes: Leaving center 19 sts free, shape opposite side of neck edge to correspond.

BACK

Work as for front through ribbing.

With MC only, repeat Row 1 of front until piece measures 14″ from beginning; end.

Armhole Shaping: Skip first 3 sts, rejoin yarn and sc across next 61 (69, 77) sts; leave remaining sts unworked.

Continuing in sc, dec 1 st each edge next row and every other row 2 times.

Work even in sc on 55 (63, 71) sts until piece measures 21″ (21½″, 22″) from beginning.

Neck Shaping: Sc across first 17 (21, 25) sts; leave remaining sts unworked.

Continuing in sc, dec 1 st at neck edge next row and every other row 1 time.

Work even in sc on 15 (19, 23) sts for 1 row.

Leaving center 21 sts free, shape opposite side of neck edge to correspond.

SLEEVES (make two)

Rib: With MC and smaller hook, ch 12.

Row 1: Sc in 2nd ch from hook and each ch across—11 sts.

Rows 2–26 (28, 30): Ch 1, turn, sc in back lp only of first st and each st across. Ch 1, work 33 (37, 41) sc evenly spaced across long edge of rib. Change to larger hook.

Body: Rows 1–5: With MC only, ch 1, turn, sc in first st and each st across.

Inc 1 st each edge next row and every 6th row 9 times.

Work even in sc on 53 (57, 61) sts until piece measures 17½″ (18″, 18½″) from beginning; end.

Shape Cap: Sk first 3 sts, rejoin yarn and sc across next 47 (51, 55) sts; leave remaining sts unworked.

Continuing in sc, dec 1 st each edge next row and every other row 2 times—41 (45, 49) sts.

Dec 1 st each edge every row until 13 sts remain.

FINISHING

With right sides facing, sew front to back at shoulder seams, sleeves to sleeve openings, sleeve and side seams.

Collar: With MC and smaller hook, start at center back and work 73 (77, 81) sc evenly spaced around neck opening; join with sl st to first sc; end.

Rib: With MC and smaller hook, ch 18.

Row 1: Sc in 2nd ch from hook and each ch across—17 sts.

Rows 2–72 (76, 80): Ch 1, turn, sc in back lp only of first st and each st across. Ch 1, work 72 (76, 80) sc evenly spaced across long edge of rib.

With right side of both pieces up, start at center front and sew collar to neck opening.

Secure and trim loose ends.

Fair Isle–style Cardigan
INTERMEDIATE

*Softly textured, subtly shaded, and stylish, this classic,
bobbled cardigan would make a versatile addition to any wardrobe.*

SIZE
Small (Medium, Large)
Finished bust: 38″ (42″, 46″)
Back length: 22″ (22½″, 23″)
Sleeve inseam: 19″ (19½″, 20″)

MATERIALS
Reynolds Kitten (brushed, worsted weight acrylic
and wool blend), 1¾ oz/160 yd balls: 8 (9, 10)
balls Lilac (MC); 1 ball each Mauve (A) and
White (B)
Sizes H and I crochet hooks (or size for gauge)
Eleven ½″ buttons

GAUGE
13 sts = 3″; 32 rows = 7″ (in pattern st)
Check gauge to assure proper fit.

SEE
Buttonholes, Chain Bobbles, Changing Color/End
of Row, Decreasing/Single Crochet, Increasing, and
Working with Chain Spaces/In

NOTE
For stitch counts, include each sc **and** each ch 1 sp

FRONT SIDE ONE

Bottom Rib: With MC and smaller hook, ch 16.
Row 1: Sc in 2nd ch from hook and each ch across—
15 sts.

Rows 2–41 (45, 49): Ch 1, turn, sc in back lp only
of first st and each st across. Ch 1, work 41 (45, 49)
sc evenly spaced across long edge of rib. Change to
larger hook.

Body: **Row 1:** Ch 1, turn, sc in first st, *ch 1, sk next
st, sc in next st*, repeat * to * across.

Row 2: Ch 1, turn, sc in first st, sc in first ch 1 sp,
ch 1, sk next st, sc in next ch 1 sp, repeat * to *
across, ending with sc in last st.

Row 3: Ch 1, turn, sc in first st, *ch 1, sk next st, sc
in next ch 1 sp*, repeat * to * across, ending with sc
in last st (rather than ch 1 sp).

Row 4: Repeat Row 2.

Row 5: With A, repeat Row 3.

Row 6: With MC, repeat Row 2.

Row 7: With B, repeat Row 3.

Row 8: With MC, repeat Row 2.

**Row 9 (wrong side; chain bobbles formed on right
side):** With A, ch 1, turn, sc in first st, *insert hook
in next st, yo, draw up a lp, ch 3, yo, draw through
both lps on hook, sc in next ch 1 sp (**ch bobble
made**)*, repeat * to * across, ending with sc in last st
(rather than ch 1 sp).

Row 10: With MC, ch 1, turn, sc in first 2 sts, *ch
1, sk next st st, sc in next st*, repeat * to * across,
ending with sc in last st.

Row 11: With B, repeat Row 3.

Row 12: With MC, repeat Row 2.

Row 13: With A, repeat Row 3.

Rows 14–18: With MC, repeat Rows 2 and 3, ending with Row 2.

Rows 19–32: Work as for Rows 5–18 **but use A when B is called for and B when A is called for.**

Repeat Rows 5–32 one time more, then repeat Rows 5–15.

Neck Shaping: With MC work Row 2 across first 32 (36, 40) sts; leave remaining sts unworked.

Next (Dec) Row: With MC, ch 1, turn, sk first st **(dec made),** sc in first ch 1 sp, *ch 1, sk next st, sc in next ch 1 sp*, repeat * to * across, ending with sc in last st (rather than ch 1 sp).

Next (Dec) Row: With MC, work as for Row 2 across, ending with sc 2 tog over last ch 1 sp and st **(dec made).**

Next (Dec) Row: With B, repeat first decrease row.

Working even on 29 (33, 37) sts, repeat Rows 20–31 (32, 32).

Sizes Medium and Large Only: With MC, repeat Row 3.

Size Large Only: With MC, repeat Rows 2 and 3 one time more.

FRONT SIDE TWO

Work as for Front Side One, reversing neck shaping.

BACK

Work rib as for front, but for 87 (95, 103) rows. Ch 1, work 87 (95, 103) sc evenly spaced across long edge of rib. Change to larger hook.

Work Rows 1–3 of front, but on 87 (95, 103) sts.

With MC only, repeat Rows 2 and 3, ending with Row 3, until piece measures 20½″ (21″, 21½″) from beginning.

Neck Shaping: Work decrease rows as for front.

Working even on 29 (33, 37) sts, repeat Rows 2 and 3 until piece measures 22″ (22½″, 23″) from beginning.

Leaving center 23 sts free, shape opposite side of neck edge to correspond.

SLEEVES (make two)

Work rib as for front, but for 35 (37, 39) rows. Ch 1, work 47 (49, 51) sc evenly spaced across long edge of rib. Change to larger hook.

With MC only, work Rows 1–3 as for front.

Row 4 (Inc Row): Ch 1, turn, sc in first st, ch 1, sc in first ch 1 sp **(inc made),** *ch 1, sk next st, sc in next ch 1 sp*, repeat * to * across, ending with ch 1, sc in last st **(inc made)**—49 (51, 53) sts.

Rows 5–8: Repeat Rows 2 and 3.

Row 9 (Inc Row): Repeat Row 4—51 (53, 55) sts.

Repeat Rows 5–9 ten (eleven, twelve) times more.

Working even on 71 (75, 79) sts, repeat Rows 2 and 3 until piece measures 19″ (19½″, 20″) from beginning.

FINISHING

With right sides facing, sew front panels to back at shoulder seams. Center sleeves at shoulder seams and sew together. Sew sleeve and side seams.

Neckband: With right side facing, MC and smaller hook, begin at center front and work 74 (78, 82) sc evenly spaced around neck opening; end.

Rib: With MC and smaller hook, ch 7.

Row 1: Sc in 2nd ch from hook and each ch across—6 sts.

Rows 2–74 (78, 82): Ch 1 turn, sc in back lp only of first st and each st across. Ch 1, work 74 (78, 82) sc evenly spaced across long edge of rib.

Starting at center front, with right sides facing, sew neckband to neck opening.

Buttonhole Band: With right side facing, MC and smaller hook work 87 sc evenly spaced along entire inner edge (bottom rib, body, and neckband) of right front; end.

Rib: Work as for neckband through Row 3.

Row 4: Ch 1, turn, sc in back lp only of first 2 sts, ch 2, sk next 2 sts, sc in back lp only of last 2 sts—**buttonhole made.**

Row 5: Ch 1, turn, sc in back lp only of first 2 sts, 2 sc in ch 2 sp, sc in back lp only of last 2 sts.

Rows 6–11: Ch 1, turn, sc in back lp only of first st and each st across.

Row 12: Repeat Row 4.

Repeat Rows 5–12 nine times more, then repeat Rows 5–7 one time—**eleven buttonholes.** Ch 1, work 87 sc evenly spaced across long edge of rib.

With right sides facing, sew buttonhole band to inner edge of right front.

Button Band: Work as for buttonhole band, but **omit buttonholes** and sew to inner edge of left front.

Finish buttonholes with buttonhole stitch and sew on buttons to correspond to buttonholes.

Secure and trim loose ends.

Tweed Stripe Vest

BEGINNER

*Single crochet spike stitch creates
the tweedy pattern in this sporty vest.*

SIZE
Small (Medium, Large)
Finished bust: 38" (42", 46")
Back length: 21½" (22", 22½")

MATERIALS
Patons Super Wool (worsted weight, machine-
washable wool), 1¾ oz/116 yd balls: 8 (9, 10)
balls Off-White (MC); 1 ball each Brown (A),
Rust (B), and Beige (C)
Sizes I and J crochet hooks (or size for gauge)

GAUGE
17 sts = 5"; 21 rows = 4" (in pattern st)
Check gauge to assure proper fit.

SEE
Changing Color/End of Row, Decreasing/Single
Crochet, Reverse Slip Stitch, Spike Stitch, and
Surface Slip Stitch

FRONT SIDE ONE

With MC and larger hook, ch 33 (37, 41).

Row 1: Sc in 2nd ch from hook and each ch across—
32 (36, 40) sts.

Row 2: Ch 1, turn, sc in first st, sc into space **below**
next st (into same place that st was worked)—**spike sc
made**—*sc in next st, spike sc in next st*, repeat * to
* across.

Rows 3–20: With MC, repeat Row 2.

Row 21: With A, repeat Row 2.

Row 22: With B, repeat Row 2.

Row 23: With C, repeat Row 2.

Rows 24–29: Repeat Rows 21–23.

Row 30: Repeat Row 21.

Repeat Rows 3–30 one time more, then Rows 3–16.

Armhole Shaping: Work Row 17 across first 29 (33,
37) sts; leave remaining sts unworked.

Next (Dec) Row: Ch 1, turn, sk first st (**dec made**),
work Row 18 across.

Next Row: Repeat Row 19.

Next (Dec) Row: Ch 1, turn, sk first st (**dec made**),
spike sc in next st, complete as for Row 20 across.

Next Row: Work as for 21 across **but** end with sc
(rather than spike sc).

Next (Dec) Row: Ch 1, turn, sk first st (**dec made**),
work Row 22 across.

Working even on 26 (30, 34) sts, repeat Rows 23–30,
then 3–13.

Neck Shaping: Work Row 14 across first 19 (23, 27)
sts; leave remaining sts unworked.

Next (Dec) Row: Ch 1, turn, sk first st (**dec made**),
work Row 15 across.

Next Row: Repeat Row 16.

Next (Dec) Row: Ch 1, turn, sk first st **(dec made)**, spike sc in next st, complete as for Row 17 across.

Next Row: Work as for Row 18 across **but** end with sc (rather than spike sc).

Next (Dec) Row: Ch 1, turn, sk first st **(dec made)**, work Row 19 across.

Working even on 16 (20, 24) sts, repeat Rows 20–30.

Sizes Medium and Large Only: Repeat Rows 3–5 (8).

FRONT SIDE TWO

Work as for Front Side One, reversing armhole and neck shaping.

BACK

With MC and larger hook, ch 65 (73, 81). Sc in 2nd ch from hook and each st across—64 (72, 80) sts.

With MC only, repeat Row 2 of front until piece measures 13½″ from beginning; end.

Armhole Shaping: Sk first 3 sts, rejoin yarn, spike sc in next st, work as for Row 2 across next 56 (64, 72) sts, sc in next st; leave remaining sts unworked.

Next (Dec) Row: Ch 1, turn, sk first st **(dec made)**, work as for Row 2 across until 2 sts remain, end as follows: insert hook below next st, yo, draw up a lp, insert hook in last st, yo, draw up a lp, yo, draw through all 3 lps on hook **(dec made)**.

Next Row: Repeat Row 2.

Next (Dec) Row: Ch 1, turn, sk first st **(dec made)**, spike sc in next st, work as for Row 2 across until 2 sts remain, end as follows: insert hook in next st, yo, draw up a lp, insert hook below next st, yo, draw up a lp, yo, draw through all 3 lps on hook **(dec made)**.

Next Row: Ch 1, turn, spike sc in first st, work as for Row 2 across **but** end with sc (rather than spike sc).

Next (Dec) Row: Repeat first decrease row.

Working even on 52 (60, 68) sts, repeat Row 2 until piece measures 20″ (20½″, 21″) from beginning.

Neck Shaping: Work Row 2 across first first 18 (22, 26) sts; leave remaining sts unworked.

Next (Dec) Row: Ch 1, turn, sk first st **(dec made)**, spike sc in next st, complete as for Row 2 across.

Next Row: Work as for Row 2 across **but** end with sc (rather than spike sc).

Next (Dec) Row: Ch 1, sk first st **(dec made)**, work Row 2 across.

Working even on 16 (20, 24) sts, repeat Row 2 until piece measures 21½″ (22″, 22½″) from beginning.

Leaving center 16 sts free, shape opposite side of neck edge to correspond.

FINISHING

With right sides facing, sew front panels to back at shoulder and side seams.

Edging: With right side facing, MC and smaller hook, start at side seam and work 1 rnd sc around entire garment edge (bottom, center front, and neckline), **working 3 sc at each corner;** join with sl st to first sc. Ch 1, don't turn, work 1 rnd reverse sl st into previous rnd; join with sl st to first reverse sl st. Ch 1, don't turn, working **below** previous rnd, work 1 rnd surface sl st around posts of first edging rnd; join with sl st to first sl st. Repeat the last rnd 1 time more; end.

Finish armhole edges in same manner.

Secure and trim loose ends.

Geometric Vest
INTERMEDIATE

Softly sensational pastel colors shine through
the geometry of a quilt-inspired, quick-to-complete vest.

SIZE
Small (Medium, Large)
Finished bust: 38" (43", 48")
Back length: 22" (22½", 23")

MATERIALS
Berroco Juliet (worsted weight mohair, acrylic, and
polyester blend), 1¾ oz/108 yd balls: 4 (5, 6) balls
Blue (MC); 3 (3, 4) balls White (CC)
Sizes J and K crochet hooks (or size for gauge)

GAUGE
10 sts = 3"; 28 rows = 9" (in pattern st)
Check gauge to assure proper fit.

SEE
Changing Color/End of Row and Within a Row,
and Decreasing/Single Crochet

FRONT/BACK (make two)

Bottom Rib: With MC and smaller hook, ch 12.

Row 1: Sc in 2nd ch from hook and each ch across—
11 sts.

Rows 2–63 (72, 81): Ch 1, turn, sc in back lp only
of first st and each st across. Ch 1, work 63 (72, 81)
sc evenly spaced across long edge of rib; end. Change
to larger hook. With right side facing, join CC.

Body: **Row 1:** With CC, sc in first 8 sts; with MC, sc
in next st, *with CC, sc in next 8 sts; with MC, sc in
next st*, repeat * to * across.

Row 2: Ch 1, turn, with MC, sc in first 2 sts; with
CC, sc in next 7 sts, *with MC, sc in next 2 sts; with
CC, sc in next 7 sts*, repeat * to * across.

Row 3: Ch 1, turn, with CC, sc in first 6 sts; with
MC, sc in next 3 sts, *with CC, sc in next 6 sts; with
MC, sc in next 3 sts*, repeat * to * across.

Row 4: Ch 1, turn, with MC, sc in first 4 sts; with
CC, sc in next 5 sts, *with MC, sc in next 4 sts; with
CC, sc in next 5 sts*, repeat * to * across.

Row 5: Ch 1, turn, with CC, sc in first 4 sts; with
MC, sc in next 5 sts, *with CC, sc in next 4 sts; with
MC, sc in next 5 sts*, repeat * to * across.

Row 6: Ch 1, turn, with MC, sc in first 6 sts; with
CC, sc in next 3 sts, *with MC, sc in next 6 sts; with
CC, sc in next 3 sts*, repeat * to * across.

Row 7: Ch 1, turn, with CC, sc in first 2 sts; with
MC, sc in next 7 sts, *with CC, sc in next 2 sts; with
MC, sc in next 7 sts*, repeat * to * across.

Row 8: Ch 1, turn, with MC, sc in first 8 sts; with
CC, sc in next st, *with MC, sc in next 8 sts; with
CC, sc in next st*, repeat * to * across.

Repeat Rows 1–8 three times more, then Rows 1–4;
end.

Armhole Shaping: Sk first 5 sts, keeping to color pattern as established, work across next 53 (62, 71) sts; leave remaining sts unworked.

Continuing to keep to established color pattern, dec 1 st each edge every row 4 times.

Working even on 45 (54, 63) sts, repeat Rows 2–8, then Rows 1–8 one time; end.

Neckband: With MC and smaller hook, ch 8 (10, 12).

Row 1: Sc in 2nd ch from hook and each ch across— 7 (9, 11) sts.

Rows 2–45 (54, 63): Ch 1, turn, sc in back lp only of first st and each st across. Ch 1, work 45 (54, 63) sc evenly spaced across long edge of rib.

With right sides facing, sew long edge of neckband to top edge of front/back.

FINISHING

On top of neckband, mark st 2″ (3″, 4″) in from armhole edge, on each side of both front and back. With right sides facing, sew shoulder seams to markers and side seams together.

Armhole Band: With right side facing, MC and smaller hook, start at side seam and work 55 (59, 63) sc evenly spaced around armhole opening; join with sl st to first sc; end.

Rib: With MC and smaller hook, ch 5.

Row 1: Sc in 2nd ch from hook and each ch across— 4 sts.

Rows 2–55 (59, 63): Ch 1, turn, sc in back lp only of first st and each st across. Ch 1, work 55 (59, 63) sc evenly spaced across long edge of rib.

With right sides facing, start at side seam and sew armhole band to armhole opening and short edges of armhole band together.

Repeat other side.

Secure and trim loose ends.

Plaid Crewneck Pullover

INTERMEDIATE

*A simple white sweater turns to windowpane plaid when
a contrasting color is slip-stitched over its surface.*

SIZE

Small (Medium, Large)
Finished bust: 38″ (41″, 46″)
Back length: 23″ (23½″, 24″)
Sleeve inseam: 19″ (19½″, 20″)

MATERIALS

Unger Utopia (worsted weight acrylic), 3½ oz/240
   yd balls: 6 (6, 7) balls White (MC); 1 ball Pink
   (CC)
Sizes I and J crochet hooks (or size for gauge)

GAUGE

14 sts = 4″; 16 rows = 4″ (in pattern st)
Check gauge to assure proper fit.

SEE

Decreasing/Single Crochet, Increasing, and Surface
Slip Stitch

NOTE

Plaid is added after front is completed

FRONT

Bottom Rib: With MC and smaller hook, ch 13.

Row 1: Sc in 2nd ch from hook and each ch across—
12 sts.

Rows 2–66 (72, 80): Ch 1, turn, sc in back lp only
of first st and each st across. Ch 1, work 66 (72, 80)
sc evenly spaced across long edge of rib. Change to
larger hook.

Body: **Rows 1–68:** With MC only, ch 1, turn, sc in
first st and each st across.

Neck Shaping: Sc across first 26 (29, 33) sts; leave
remaining sts unworked.

Continuing in sc, dec 1 st at neck edge next row and
every other row 2 times.

Work even in sc on 23 (26, 30) sts for 6 (8, 10) rows.

Leaving center 14 sts free, shape opposite side of neck
edge to correspond.

BACK

Work as for front through Body Row 1.

Repeat Row 1 until piece measures 21½″ (22″, 22½″)
from beginning.

Neck Shaping: Shape neckline as for front but work
even in sc on 23 (26, 30) sts for only 1 row [rather
than 6 (8, 10)].

SLEEVES (make two)

Work rib as for front but for 28 (30, 32) rows. Ch 1,
work 28 (30, 32) sc evenly spaced across long edge of
rib. Change to larger hook.

Row 1: With MC only, ch 1, turn, sc in first 2 (3, 4)
sts, 2 sc in next st **(inc made)**, *sc in next 3 sts, 2 sc
in next st **(inc made)***, repeat * to * across, ending
with sc in last 1 (2, 3) sts—35 (37, 39) sts.

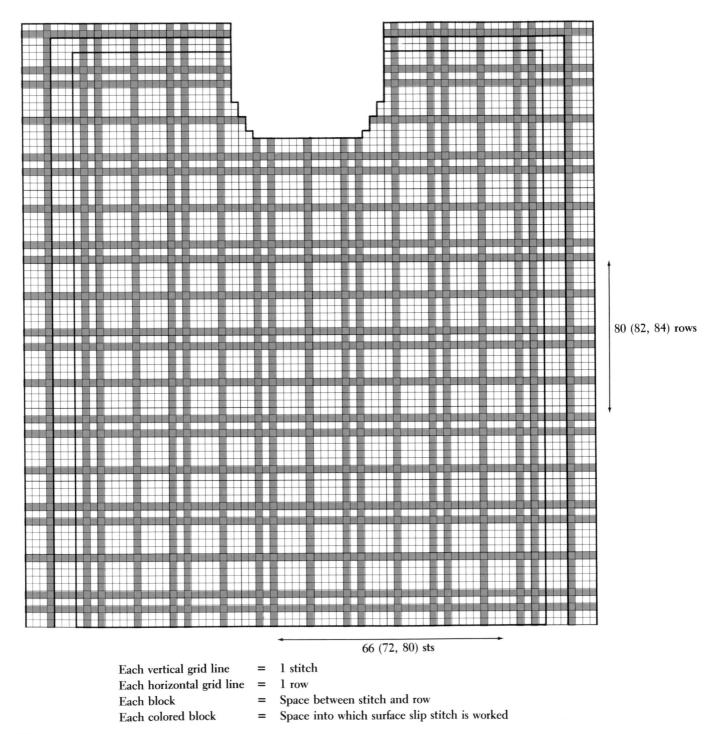

80 (82, 84) rows

66 (72, 80) sts

Each vertical grid line	=	1 stitch
Each horizontal grid line	=	1 row
Each block	=	Space between stitch and row
Each colored block	=	Space into which surface slip stitch is worked

Rows 2–6: Ch 1, turn, sc in first st and each st across.

Continuing in sc, inc 1 st each edge next row and every 6th row (8, 9, 10) times.

Work even in sc on 53 (57, 61) sts until piece measures 19″ (19½″, 20″) from beginning.

PLAID

Plaid is worked **between** stitches with surface slip stitch. Yarn is held at back of work throughout. It is important that stitch tension be neither too tight nor too loose, and that a sufficient length of yarn be left at **each** end to secure later. **Refer to diagram.** With right side of front facing, CC and smaller hook, begin the first vertical plaid line as follows: Count over 2 (5, 4) sts from **your** right, insert hook, **from front to back,** into space between 2nd and 3rd (5th and 6th, 4th and 5th) sts horizontally and **below** Row 1 (**between** rib edging row and first row) vertically. Holding yarn at back of work, yo, draw up a lp; *insert hook in sp directly above sp just worked, yo, draw up a lp and draw that lp through the lp on hook*, repeat * to * to shoulder seam.

Count over 2 (2, 5) sts and work the next vertical plaid line in the same manner. Work remaining vertical lines, following diagram, across the garment.

Then, continuing to follow the diagram, work the horizontal plaid lines in the same manner, starting at the edge to **your** right and working around posts, into spaces **between** rows.

FINISHING

With right sides facing, sew front to back at shoulder seams. Center sleeves at shoulder seams and sew together. Sew sleeve and side seams.

Neckband: With MC and smaller hook, start at center back and work 65 (69, 73) sc evenly spaced around neck opening; join with sl st to first sc; end.

Rib: With MC and smaller hook, ch 6.

Row 1: Sc in 2nd ch from hook and each ch across— 5 sts.

Rows 2–65 (69, 73): Ch 1, turn, sc in back lp only of first st and each st across. Ch 1, work 65 (69, 73) sc evenly spaced across long edge of rib.

Starting at center back, with right sides facing, sew neckband to neck opening and short edges of neckband together.

Secure and trim loose ends.

Double and Single
Crochet Combination Patterns

Block Pattern Pullover
INTERMEDIATE

Soft gray, mauve, pink, and white are used with subtle sophistication to give this geometrically patterned sweater a contemporary elegance.

SIZE
Small (Medium, Large)
Finished bust: 38″ (42″, 48″)
Back length: 22″ (22½″, 23″)
Sleeve inseam: 19″ (19½″, 20″)

MATERIALS
Reynolds Kitten (brushed, worsted weight acrylic and wool blend), 1¾ oz/160 yd balls: 7 (7, 8) balls Gray (MC); 1 (1, 2) balls each Mauve (A), Pink (B) and White (C)
Size G crochet hook (or size for gauge)

GAUGE
32 sts = 7″, 11 rows = 5″ (in pattern st)
Check gauge to assure proper fit.

SEE
Changing Color/End of Row and Within a Row, Decreasing/Double Crochet, and Increasing

FRONT

Bottom Rib: With MC, ch 16.

Row 1: Sc in 2nd ch from hook and each ch across—15 sts.

Rows 2–87 (97, 109): Ch 1, turn, sc in back lp only of first st and each st across. Ch 1, work 87 (97, 109) sc evenly spaced across long edge of rib.

Body: **Row 1 (wrong side):** With MC, ch 3 (for first dc), turn, sk first st, dc in each st across.

Rows 2–3: With MC, ch 3 (for first dc), turn, sk first st, dc in next 2 (1, 1) sts; with A, dc in next 3 sts; *with MC, dc in next 3 sts; with A, dc in next 3 sts*, repeat * to * across, ending with MC dc in last 3 (2, 2) sts.

Rows 4–5: With B, ch 3 (for first dc), turn, sk first st, dc in next 2 (1, 1) sts; with MC, dc in next 3 sts; *with B, dc in next 3 sts; with MC, dc in next 3 sts*, repeat * to * across, ending with B dc in last 3 (2, 2) sts.

Rows 6–7: With MC, ch 3 (for first dc), turn, sk first st, dc in next 2 (1, 1) sts; with C, dc in next 3 sts; *with MC, dc in next 3 sts; with C, dc in next 3 sts*, repeat * to * across, ending with MC dc in last 3 (2, 2) sts.

Rows 8–9: With A, ch 3 (for first dc), turn, sk first st, dc in next 2 (1, 1) sts; with MC, dc in next 3 sts; *with A, dc in next 3 sts; with MC, dc in next 3 sts*, repeat * to * across, ending with A dc in last 3 (2, 2) sts.

Rows 10–11: With MC, ch 3 (for first dc), turn, sk first st, dc in next 2 (1, 1) sts; *with MC, dc in next 3 sts; with B, dc in next 3 sts*, repeat * to * across, ending with MC dc in last 3 (2, 2) sts.

Rows 12–13: With C, ch 3 (for first dc), turn, sk first st, dc in next 2 (1, 1) sts; with MC, dc in next 3 sts; *with C, dc in next 3 sts; with MC, dc in next 3 sts*, repeat * to * across, ending with C dc in last 3 (2, 2) sts.

Repeat Rows 2–13 one time more, then Rows 2–3.

Armhole Shaping: Skip first 9 sts, rejoin yarn and work Row 10 across next 69 (79, 91) sts; leave remaining sts unworked.

Working even on 69 (79, 91) sts, repeat Rows 11–13, then Rows 2–7.

Neck Shaping: Work Row 8 across first 25 (30, 36) sts, dc 2 tog over next 2 sts (**dec made**); leave remaining sts unworked.

Keeping to color block pattern, as established, dec 1 st at neck edge every row 2 times.

Work even on 24 (29, 35) sts for 4 (5, 6) rows.

Leaving center 15 sts free, shape opposite side of neck edge to correspond.

BACK

Work as for front through armhole shaping.

Working even on 69 (79, 91) sts, repeat Rows 11–13, then 2–11 (12, 13).

Neck Shaping: Work Row 12 (13, 2) across first 24 (29, 35) sts, dc 2 tog over next 2 sts (**dec made**); leave remaining sts unworked.

Keeping to color block pattern, as established, dec 1 st at neck edge next row.

Work even on 24 (29, 35) sts for 1 row.

Leaving center 17 sts free, shape opposite side of neck edge to correspond.

SLEEVES (make two)

Work rib as for front but for 30 (32, 34) rows. Ch 1, turn, work 30 (32, 34) sc evenly spaced across long edge of rib.

Row 1: With MC only, ch 3 (for first dc), turn, skip first st, dc in next 6 (7, 8) sts, 2 dc in next st (**inc made**), *dc in next 7 sts, 2 dc in next st (**inc made**),* repeat * to * across, ending with dc in last 6 (7, 8) sts—33 (35, 37) sts.

Row 2: Ch 3 (for first dc), turn, sk first st, dc in each st across.

Continuing in dc, inc 1 st each edge next row and every other row 15 (16, 17) times.

Work even in dc on 65 (69, 73) sts until piece measures 21″ (21½″, 22″) from beginning.

FINISHING

With right sides facing, sew front to back at shoulder seams, sleeves to sleeve openings, sleeve and side seams.

Neckband: With right side facing and MC, begin at center back and work 76 (80, 84) sc evenly spaced around neck opening; join with sl st to first sc; end.

Rib: With MC, ch 7.

Row 1: Sc in 2nd ch from hook and each ch across—6 sts.

Rows 2–76 (80, 84): Ch 1, turn, sc in back lp only of first st and each st across. Ch 1, work 76 (80, 84) sc evenly spaced across long edge of rib.

Starting at center back, with right sides facing, sew neckband to neck opening and short edges of neckband together.

Secure and trim loose ends.

Openwork Pullover
INTERMEDIATE

Short sleeves, lightweight yarn, and airy openwork make this perfect for summer wear.

SIZE
Small (Medium, Large)
Finished bust: 40″ (44″, 47″)
Back length: 23″ (23½″, 24″)

MATERIALS
Phildar Prognostic (sport weight acrylic and wool blend), 1¾ oz/175 yd balls: 6 (7, 8) balls in color of choice
Size F crochet hook (or size for gauge)

GAUGE
36 sts = 7″; 12 rows = 4″ (in pattern st)
Check gauge to assure proper fit.

SEE
Decreasing/Double Crochet and Single Crochet, and Working with Chain Spaces/In

FRONT

Bottom Rib: Ch 16.

Row 1: Sc in 2nd ch from hook and each ch across—15 sts.

Rows 2–102 (112, 122): Ch 1, turn, sc in back lp only of first st and each st across. Ch 1, work 102 (112, 122) sc evenly spaced across long edge of rib.

Body: **Begin Border Chart (see diagram),** working Row 1 as follows: **A to B:** Ch 3 (for first dc), turn, sk first st, dc in next 4 sts, *ch 2, sk next 2 sts, dc in next 7 (8, 9) sts*, repeat * to * 4 times more, ch 1, sk 1

st; **B to A:** Ch 1, sk 1 st, *dc in next 7 (8, 9) sts, ch 2, sk 2 sts*, repeat * to * 4 times more, end with dc in last 5 sts (**Row 1 of chart completed**).

Work Row 2 of chart as follows: **A to B:** Ch 3 (for first dc), turn, sk first st, dc in next 2 sts, *ch 2, sk 2 sts, 2 dc in ch 2 sp, dc in next 5 (6, 7) sts*, repeat * to * 4 times more, ch 2, sk 2 sts, 1 dc in ch 2 sp; **B to A:** 1 dc in ch 2 sp, ch 2, sk 2 sts, *dc in next 5 (6, 7) sts, 2 dc in ch 2 sp, ch 2, sk 2 sts*, repeat * to * 4 times more, end with dc in last 3 sts.

In the same manner, work Rows 3–25 (28, 30) of chart.

Size Small Only: Work even in dc for 1 row.

All Sizes: **Begin Center Chart (see diagram),** working Row 1 as follows: Ch 3 (for first dc), turn, sk first st, dc in next 49 (54, 59) sts, ch 2, sk 2 sts, dc in last 50 (55, 60) sts.

In the same manner, work Rows 2–17 of chart.

Work even in dc for 3 (3, 2) rows.

Neck Shaping: Ch 3 (for first dc), turn, sk first st, dc in next 38 (42, 46) sts; leave remaining sts unworked.

Continuing in dc, dec 1 st at neck edge every row 4 times.

Work even in dc on 35 (39, 43) sts until piece measures 23 (23½″, 24″) from beginning.

Leaving center 24 (26, 28) sts free, shape opposite side of neck edge to correspond.

BORDER CHART

Work A to B one time, then B to A one time

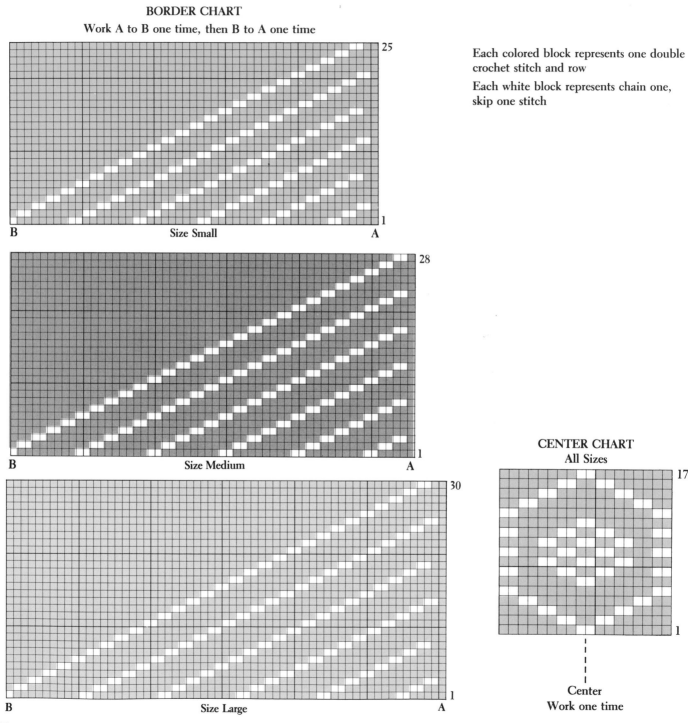

Each colored block represents one double crochet stitch and row

Each white block represents chain one, skip one stitch

25

B   Size Small   A

28

B   Size Medium   A

30

B   Size Large   A

CENTER CHART
All Sizes

17

1

Center
Work one time

BACK

Work as for front through ribbing.

Body: **Row 1:** Ch 3 (for first dc), turn, sk first st, dc in each st across.

Repeat Row 1 until piece measures 22″ (22½″, 23″) from beginning.

Neck Shaping: Ch 3 (for first dc), turn, sk first st, dc in next 35 (39, 43) sts; leave remaining sts unworked.

Continuing in dc, dec 1 st at neck edge next row.

Work even in dc on 35 (39, 43) sts for 1 row.

Leaving center 30 (32, 34) sts free, shape opposite side of neck edge to correspond.

FINISHING

With right sides facing, sew front to back at shoulder seams.

Neckband: With right side facing, start at center back and work 105 (109, 113) sc evenly spaced around neck opening; join with sl st to first sc; end.

Rib: Ch 7.

Row 1: Sc in 2nd ch from hook and each ch across— 6 sts.

Rows 2–105 (109, 113): Ch 1, turn, sc in back lp only of first st and each st across. Ch 1, work 105 (109, 113) sc evenly spaced across long edge of rib.

Starting at center back, with right sides facing, sew neckband to neck opening and short edges of neckband together.

Armhole Bands: On both front and back, mark st 7½″ (8″, 8½″) down from shoulder seam. With right side facing, work 85 (89, 93) sc evenly spaced between markers. Ch 1, turn, sc in first 4 (6, 8) sts, sc 2 tog **(dec made)**, *sc in next 3 sts, sc 2 tog **(dec made)***, repeat * to * across, ending with sc in last 4 (6, 8) sts—69 (73, 77) sts; end.

Rib: Work as for neckband but for 69 (73, 77) rows. Ch 1, work 69 (73, 77) sc evenly spaced across long edge of rib.

With right sides facing, sew rib to armhole edge.

Repeat other side.

Sew side seams.

Secure and trim loose ends.

Wavy Shell Pattern Pullover Vest

BEGINNER

*A classically casual vest in shades of gray,
wine, and cream — perfect to wear indoors or out.*

SIZE

Small (Medium, Large)
Finished bust: 38″ (42″, 46″)
Back length: 21½″ (22″, 22½″)

MATERIALS

Patons Super Wool (worsted weight, machine-
washable wool), 1¾ oz/116 yd balls: 6 (7, 8) balls
Gray (MC); 2 balls each Wine (A) and Cream (B)
Size H crochet hook (or size for gauge)

GAUGE

16 sts = 4″; 8 rows = 4″ (in pattern st)
Check gauge to assure proper fit.

SEE:

Changing Color/End of Row and Decreasing/
Double Crochet

FRONT

Bottom Rib: With MC, ch 14.

Row 1: Sc in 2nd ch from hook and each ch across—
13 sts.

Rows 2–76 (84, 92): Ch 1, turn, sc in back lp only
of first st and each st across. Ch 1, work 76 (84, 92)
sc evenly spaced across long edge of rib.

Body: **Row 1:** Ch 3 (for first dc), turn, sk first st, dc
in next 3 sts, *sc in next 4 sts, dc in next 4 sts*, repeat
* to * across.

Rows 2–3: With A, ch 1, turn, sc in first 4 sts, *dc
in next 4 sts, sc in next 4 sts*, repeat * to * across.

Rows 4–5: With B, repeat Row 1.

Rows 6–7: With MC, repeat Row 2.

Rows 8–9: With A, repeat Row 1.

Rows 10–11: With B, repeat Row 2.

Rows 12–13: With MC, repeat Row 1.

Repeat Rows 2–13 one time more, then Rows 2–6
(shell pattern ends).

With MC only, ch 3 (for first dc), turn, sk first st, dc
in each st across; end.

Armhole Shaping: Sk first 6 (7, 7) sts, rejoin yarn in
next st, ch 3 (for first dc), dc in next 63 (69, 77) sts;
leave remaining sts unworked.

Continuing in dc, dec 1 st each edge every row 3
times.

Work even in dc on 58 (64, 72) sts for 1 (2, 3) rows.

Neck Shaping: Dc across first 17 (20, 23) sts; leave
remaining sts unworked.

Continuing in dc, dec 1 st at neck edge every row 3
times.

Work even in dc on 14 (17, 20) sts for 7 rows.

Leaving center 24 (24, 26) sts free, shape opposite side
of neck edge to correspond.

BACK

Work as for front through armhole shaping.

Work even in dc on 58 (64, 72) sts for 9 (10, 11) rows.

Neck Shaping: Dc across first 15 (18, 21) sts; leave remaining sts unworked.

Continuing in dc, dec 1 st at neck edge next row.

Work even in dc on 14 (17, 20) sts for 1 row.

Leaving center 28 (28, 30) sts free, shape opposite side of neck edge to correspond.

FINISHING

With right sides facing, sew front to back at shoulder and side seams.

Neckband: With right side facing and MC, start at center back and work 102 (102, 106) sc evenly spaced around neck opening; join with sl st to first sc; end.

Rib: With MC, ch 6.

Row 1: Sc in 2nd ch from hook and each ch across—5 sts.

Rows 2–102 (102, 106): Ch 1, turn, sc in back lp only of first st and each st across. Ch 1, work 102 (102, 106) sc evenly spaced across long edge of rib.

Starting at center back, with right sides facing, sew neckband to neck opening and short edges of neckband together.

Armhole Bands: With right side facing and MC, start at side seam and work 73 (77, 81) sc evenly spaced around armhole opening; join with sl st to first sc; end.

Rib: Work as for neckband but for 73 (77, 81) rows. Ch 1, work 73 (77, 81) sc evenly spaced across long edge of rib.

With right sides facing, start at side seam and sew armhole band to armhole opening and short edges of armhole band together.

Repeat other side.

Secure and trim loose ends.

Long Vest with Wavy Shell Pattern

INTERMEDIATE

*Rich southwestern colors cascade down
the front of this open vest.*

SIZE

Small (Medium, Large)
Finished bust: 38″ (42″, 46″)
Back length: 28″

MATERIALS

Pingouin Le Yarn 3 (worsted weight acrylic, wool, and polypropylene blend), 3½ oz/200 yd balls: 4 (5, 5) balls Brown (MC); 1 ball each Red (A) and Cream (B)
Size H crochet hook (or size for gauge)

GAUGE:

13 sts = 4″; 9 rows = 5″ (in pattern st)
Check gauge to assure proper fit.

SEE

Changing Color/End of Row, Decreasing/Double Crochet, Increasing, Reverse Slip Stitch, and Surface Slip Stitch

NOTE

Garment is worked from side to side, rather than from hem to shoulder

FRONT SIDE ONE

With MC, ch 64 (63, 62).

First Row: Dc in 4th ch from hook and each ch across—62 (61, 60) sts.

Next Row: Ch 3 (for first dc), turn, sk first st, dc in each st across.

Repeat the last row 3 (4, 4) times more.

Armhole Shaping: Ch 1, turn, sc in first st and each st across; with a separate strand of MC, ch 29 (30, 31); sc in each new ch—91 sts.

Size Large Only: Work even in dc for 1 row.

All Sizes: Stripe Pattern: Row 1: Ch 3 (for first dc), turn, sk first st, dc in next 6 sts, *sc in next 7 sts, dc in next 7 sts*, repeat * to * across.

Row 2: With A, ch 1, turn, sc in first st and each st across.

Row 3: With B, ch 1, turn, sl st in first 7 sts, *dc in next 7 sts, sl st in next 7 sts*, repeat * to * across.

Row 4: With B, repeat Row 2.

Row 5: Repeat Row 3.

Row 6: With MC, repeat Row 2.

Row 7: With A, ch 3 (for first dc), turn, sk first st, dc in next 6 sts, *sl st in next 7 sts, dc in next 7 sts*, repeat * to * across.

Row 8: With A, repeat Row 2.

Row 9: Repeat Row 7.

Row 10: Repeat Row 6.

Rows 11–13: Repeat Rows 3–5.

Row 14: Repeat Row 2.

Row 15: With MC, repeat Row 1 (**stripe pattern ends**).

Size Large Only: With MC, work even in dc for 1 row.

All Sizes: With MC only, work even in sc for 1 row; end.

Neck Shaping: Sk first 12 (12, 13) sts, rejoin yarn in next st, ch 2 (**dec made**), dc in next st and each st across—78 (78, 77) sts.

Continuing in dc, dec 1 st at neck edge every row 2 times.

Work even in dc on 76 (76, 75) sts for 1 (2, 2) rows.

FRONT SIDE TWO

Work as for Front Side One to armhole shaping.

Armhole Shaping: Ch 30 (31, 32), turn, sc in 2nd ch from hook, in each new ch and each st across—91 sts.

Work as for Front Side One to neck shaping **but don't end.**

Neck Shaping: Ch 3 (for first dc), turn, sk first st, dc in next 76 (76, 75) sts, dc 2 tog over next 2 sts (**dec made**); leave remaining sts unworked—78 (78, 77) sts.

Complete as for Front Side One.

BACK

Work as for Front Side One to armhole shaping.

Armhole Shaping: With MC only, ch 31 (32, 33), turn, dc in 4th ch from hook, in each new ch and each st across.

Work even in dc on 91 sts for 7 (7, 9) rows; end.

Neck Shaping: Sk first 5 sts, rejoin yarn in next st, ch 2 (**dec made**), dc in next st and each st across—85 sts.

Continuing in dc, dec 1 st at neck edge next row.

Work even in dc on 84 sts for 4 (6, 6) rows.

Continuing in dc, inc 1 st at neck edge every row 2 times—86 sts.

Next Row: Ch 7, turn, dc in 4th ch from hook, in each new ch and each st across.

Work even in dc on 91 sts for 7 (7, 9) rows; end.

Armhole Shaping: Sk first 29 (30, 31) sts, rejoin yarn in next st, ch 3 (for first dc), dc in next st and each st across.

Work even in dc on 62 (61, 60) sts for 4 (5, 5) rows.

FINISHING

With right sides facing, sew front to back at shoulder and side seams.

Edging: With right side facing and MC, start at side seam and work 1 rnd sc around entire garment edge (bottom, center front, and neckline), **working 3 sc at each corner**; join with sl st to first sc. Ch 1, don't turn, work 1 rnd reverse sl st into previous rnd; join with sl st to first reverse sl st. Ch 1, don't turn, working **below** previous rnd, work 1 rnd surface sl st around posts of first edging rnd; join with sl st to first sl st. Repeat the last rnd 1 time more; end.

Finish armhole edges in same manner.

Secure and trim loose ends.

Fair Isle–style Vest

INTERMEDIATE

Wear this sumptuous mohair vest over a sparkling white turtleneck on a snowy winter afternoon.

SIZE

Small (Medium, Large)
Finished bust: 38″ (41″, 45″)
Back length: 21½″ (22″, 22½″)

MATERIALS

Classic Elite La Gran Mohair (worsted weight mohair, wool, and nylon blend), 1½ oz/90 yd balls: 8 (9, 10) balls Blue (MC); 2 balls Cream (CC)
Size I crochet hook (or size for gauge)

GAUGE

10 sts = 3″; 7 rows = 4″ (in pattern st)
Check gauge to assure proper fit.

SEE

Changing Color/End of Row and Within a Row, and Decreasing/Double Crochet

FRONT

Bottom Rib: With MC, ch 12.

Row 1: Sc in 2nd ch from hook and each ch across—11 sts.

Rows 2–63 (69, 75): Ch 1, turn, sc in back lp only of first st and each st across. Ch 1, work 63 (69, 75) sc evenly spaced across long edge of rib.

Body: **Row 1 (wrong side):** With CC, ch 3 (for first dc), turn, sk first st, dc in each st across.

Row 2: With CC, ch 3 (for first dc), turn, sk first st, dc in next 2 sts; *with MC, dc in next 3 sts; with CC, dc in next 3 sts*, repeat * to * across.

Row 3: With MC, ch 3 (for first dc), turn, sk first st, dc in next 2 sts; *with CC, dc in next 3 sts; with MC, dc in next 3 sts*, repeat * to * across.

Row 4: Repeat Row 2.

Row 5: Repeat Row 1.

Row 6: With MC, repeat Row 1.

Row 7: Repeat Row 3.

Row 8: Repeat Row 6.

Repeat Rows 1–8 one time more, then Row 1; end.

Armhole Shaping: Sk first 6 sts, rejoin yarn and work Row 2 across next 51 (57, 63) sts; leave remaining sts unworked.

Keeping to color block pattern, as established, dec 1 st each edge every row 3 times.

Working even on 45 (51, 57) sts, repeat Rows 6, 2, 8, then 1.

Neck Shaping: Work Row 3 across first 15 (18, 21) sts; leave remaining sts unworked.

Keeping to color block pattern, as established, dec 1 st at neck edge every row 3 times.

Work even on 12 (15, 18) sts for 3 (4, 5) rows.

Leaving center 15 sts free, shape opposite side of neck edge to correspond.

BACK

Work as for front through ribbing.

Body: Rows 1–17: With MC only, repeat Row 1 of front; end.

Armhole Shaping: Sk first 6 sts, rejoin yarn, dc across next 51 (57, 63) sts; leave remaining sts unworked.

Continuing in dc, dec 1 st each edge every row 3 times.

Work even in dc on 45 (51, 57) sts for 9 (10, 11) rows.

Neck Shaping: Dc across first 11 (14, 17) sts, dc 2 tog over next 2 sts; leave remaining sts unworked.

Work even in dc on 12 (15, 18) sts for 1 row.

Leaving center 19 sts free, shape opposite side of neck edge to correspond.

FINISHING

With right sides facing, sew front to back at shoulder and side seams.

Neckband: With right side facing and MC, begin at center back and work 70 (74, 78) sc evenly spaced around neck opening; join with sl st to first sc; end.

Rib: With MC, ch 5.

Row 1: Sc in 2nd ch from hook and each ch across— 4 sts.

Rows 2–70 (74, 78): Ch 1, turn, sc in back lp only of first st and each st across. Ch 1, work 70 (74, 78) sc evenly spaced across long edge of rib.

Starting at center back, with right sides facing, sew neckband to neck opening and short edges of neckband together.

Armhole Bands: With right side facing and MC, begin at side seam and work 72 (76, 80) sc evenly spaced around armhole opening; join with sl st to first sc; end.

Rib: Work rib as for neckband but for 72 (76, 80) rows. Ch 1, work 72 (76, 80) sc evenly spaced across long edge of rib.

Starting at side seam, with right sides facing, sew armhole band to armhole opening and short edges of armhole band together.

Repeat other side.

Secure and trim loose ends.

Lacy Pullover
BEGINNER

The alluring chain lace panels in this solid-colored sweater
create an intricate-looking pattern that
is easy enough for a beginner.

SIZE
Small (Medium, Large)
Finished bust: 38″ (42″, 47″)
Back length: 22″
Sleeve inseam: 19″ (19½″, 20″)

MATERIALS
Reynolds Kitten (brushed, worsted weight acrylic
and wool blend), 1¾ oz/160 yd balls: 8 (9, 10)
balls in color of choice
Size G crochet hook (or size for gauge)

GAUGE
16 sts = 4″, 13 rows = 5″ (in pattern st)
Check gauge to assure proper fit.

SEE
Decreasing/Double Crochet, Increasing, and Working with Chain Spaces/In

FRONT

Bottom Rib: Ch 16.

Row 1: Sc in 2nd ch from hook and each ch across—
15 sts.

Rows 2–76 (85, 94): Ch 1, turn, sc in back lp only
of first st and each st across. Ch 1, work 76 (85, 94)
sc evenly spaced across long edge of rib.

Body: **Rows 1–3:** Ch 3 (for first dc), turn, sk first st,
dc in next st and each st across.

Row 4: Ch 1, turn, sc in first st, *ch 3, sk next 2 sts,
sc in next st*, repeat * to * across.

Row 5: Ch 3, turn, sc in first ch 3 sp, *ch 3, sc in
next ch 3 sp*, repeat * to * across, ending with ch 1,
hdc in last st.

Row 6: Ch 1, turn, sc in first st, ch 3, sk ch 1 sp, sc
in first ch 3 sp, *ch 3, sc in next ch 3 sp*, repeat *
to * across, ending with ch 3, sc in 2nd ch of turning
ch 3 of previous row.

Row 7: Ch 3 (for first dc), turn, sk first st, 2 dc in first
ch 3 sp, *dc in next st, 2 dc in next ch 3 sp*, repeat
* to * across, ending with dc in last st.

Repeat Rows 2–7 five times more, then Rows 2–3.

Neck Shaping: Work Row 4 across first 28 (31, 34)
sts; leave remaining sts unworked.

Next (Dec) Row: Ch 1, turn, sc in first ch 3 sp (**dec
made**), *ch 3, sc in next ch 3 sp*, repeat * to * across,
ending with ch 1, hdc in last st.

Next Row: Work as for Row 6 across, **but** end with
ch 1, hdc in last st.

Next Row: Ch 3 (for first dc), turn, sk first st, dc in
ch 1 sp, dc in next st, *2 dc in next ch 3 sp, dc in
next st*, repeat * to * across.

Next (Dec) Row: Repeat Row 2, ending with dc 2 tog
over last 2 sts (**dec made**).

Next (Dec) Row: Ch 2, turn, sk first st (**dec made**), dc in next st and each st across.

Working even on 25 (28, 31) sts, repeat Rows 4–7 one time.

Leaving center 20 (23, 26) sts free, shape opposite side of neck edge to correspond.

BACK

Work as for front through Body Row 1.

Repeat Row 1 until piece measures 21″ from beginning.

Neck Shaping: Dc across first 24 (27, 30) sts, dc 2 tog over next 2 sts (**dec made**); leave remaining sts unworked.

Work even in dc on 25 (28, 31) sts for 1 row.

Leaving center 24 (27, 30) sts free, shape opposite side of neck edge to correspond.

SLEEVES (make two)

Work rib as for front but for 30 (32, 34) rows. Ch 1, work 35 (37, 39) sc evenly spaced across long edge of rib.

Work Body Row 1 of front on 35 (37, 39) sts.

Continuing in dc, inc 1 st each edge next row and every other row 12 (13, 14) times.

Work even in dc on 61 (65, 69) sts until piece measures 19″ (19½″, 20″) from beginning.

FINISHING

With right sides facing, sew front to back at shoulder seams. Center sleeves at shoulder seams and sew together. Sew sleeve and side seams.

Neckband: With right side facing, start at center back and work 79 (85, 91) sc evenly spaced around neck opening; join with sl st to first sc; end.

Rib: Ch 7.

Row 1: Sc in 2nd ch from hook and each ch across—6 sts.

Rows 2–79 (85, 91): Ch 1, turn, sc in back lp only of first st and each st across. Ch 1, work 79 (85, 91) sc evenly spaced across long edge of rib.

With right sides facing, start at center back and sew neckband to neck opening and short edges of neckband together.

Secure and trim loose ends.

Textured Turtleneck
BEGINNER

An oversized, seed-patterned turtleneck provides the perfect protection from whistling winter winds.

SIZE
Small (Medium, Large)
Finished bust: 40″ (44″, 48″)
Back length: 24″ (24½″, 25″)
Sleeve inseam: 17½″ (18″, 18½″)

MATERIALS
Brunswick Windmist (brushed, worsted weight Orlon acrylic), 1¾ oz/135 yd balls: 11 (13, 14) balls in color of choice
Sizes I and J crochet hooks (or size for gauge)

GAUGE
23 sts = 6″; 21 rows = 5″ (in pattern st)
Check gauge to assure proper fit.

SEE
Decreasing/Single Crochet, Increasing, and Seed Pattern

FRONT

Bottom Rib: With smaller hook, ch 16.

Row 1: Sc in 2nd ch from hook and each ch across—15 sts.

Rows 2–77 (85, 93): Ch 1, turn, sc in back lp only of first st and each st across. Ch 1, work 77 (85, 93) sc evenly spaced across long edge of rib. Change to larger hook.

Body: **Row 1:** Ch 1, turn, sc in front lp only of first st and each st across.

Row 2 (right side): Ch 1, turn, sc in both lps of first st, *sk next st current row, dc in unused lp of sc 1 row below, sc in both lps next st current row*, repeat * to * across.

Row 3: Repeat Row 1.

Row 4: Ch 1, turn, sk first st current row, dc in unused lp of sc 1 row below, *sc in both lps next st current row, sk next st current row, dc in unused lp of sc 1 row below*, repeat * to * across.

Repeat Rows 1–4, ending with Row 4, until piece measures 16″ from beginning; end.

Armhole Shaping: Sk first 4 sts, rejoin yarn and work Row 1 across next 69 (77, 85) sts; leave remaining sts unworked.

Next Row: Repeat Row 2.

Next Row: Decreasing 1 st each edge, repeat Row 1.
Repeat the last 2 rows 3 times more.

Working even on 61 (69, 77) sts, repeat Rows 2–4, then Rows 1–4 one time.

Neck Shaping: Work Row 1 across first 23 (27, 31) sts; leave remaining sts unworked.

Next Row: Repeat Row 2.

Next Row: Repeat Row 1, ending with sc 2 tog (**dec made**).

Next Row: Work as for Row 2 across **but** end with dc in unused lp of sc 1 row below (rather than sc).

Next Row: Repeat the first decrease row.

Repeat the last 4 rows 1 time more.

Working even on 19 (23, 27) sts, repeat rows 2–4, then Rows 1–4, ending with right side row, until piece measures 24″ (24½″, 25″) from beginning.

Leaving center 15 sts free, shape opposite side of neck edge to correspond.

BACK

Work as for front through ribbing.

Body: **Row 1:** Ch 1, turn, sc in front lp only of first st and each st across.

Row 2 (right side): Ch 1, turn, sc in both lps of first st and each st across.

Repeat Rows 1–2, ending with Row 2, until piece measures 16″ from beginning; end.

Armhole Shaping: Sk first 4 sts, rejoin yarn and work Row 1 across next 69 (77, 85) sts; leave remaining sts unworked.

Keeping to row pattern, as established, dec 1 st each edge next row and every other row 3 times.

Working even on 61 (69, 77) sts repeat Rows 1–2, ending with Row 2, until piece measures 22½″ (23″, 23½″) from beginning.

Neck Shaping: Work Row 1 across first 22 (26, 30) sts; leave remaining sts unworked.

Keeping to row pattern, dec 1 st at neck edge next row and every other row 2 times—19 (23, 27) sts.

Leaving center 17 sts free, shape opposite side of neck edge to correspond.

SLEEVES (make two)

Work rib as for front but for 29 (31, 33) rows. Ch 1, work 43 (47, 51) sc evenly spaced across long edge of rib. Change to large hook.

Rows 1–5: Repeat Rows 1–2 of back, ending with Row 1.

Keeping to row pattern, as established, inc 1 st each edge next row and every 6th row 8 times.

Working even on 61 (65, 69) sts, repeat Rows 1–2, ending with Row 2, until piece measures 17½″ (18″, 18½″) from beginning; end.

Shape Cap: Sk first 4 sts, rejoin yarn and work Row 1 across next 53 (57, 61) sts; leave remaining sts unworked.

Work decrease rows as for back armhole shaping—45 (49, 53) sts.

Decreasing 1 st each edge **every** row, repeat Rows 1–2 until 21 sts remain.

FINISHING

With right sides facing, sew front to back at shoulder seams, sleeves to sleeve openings, sleeve and side seams.

Collar: With right side facing and smaller hook, start at center back and work 76 (80, 84) sc evenly spaced around neck opening; join with sl st to first sc; end.

Rib: With smaller hook, ch 34.

Row 1: Sc in 2nd ch from hook and each ch across— 33 sts.

Rows 2–76 (80, 84): Ch 1, turn, sc in back lp only of first st and each st across. Ch 1, work 76 (80, 84) sc evenly spaced across long edge of rib.

Sew short edges of collar together to form tube.

With tube and sweater right side out, insert tube in neck opening, start at center back and sew together.

Secure and trim loose ends.

Texture-Patterned Pullover

INTERMEDIATE

*Breeze through summer with sun-drenched style
in this lemon yellow shell.*

SIZE

Small (Medium, Large)
Finished bust: 38″ (42″, 45″)
Back length: 22″ (22½″, 23″)

MATERIALS

Patons SuperSoft (sport weight acrylic), 1⅓ oz/153
  yd balls: 8 (9, 10) balls in color of choice
Sizes G and H crochet hooks (or size for gauge)

GAUGE

18 sts = 4″; 19 rows = 4″ (in pattern st)
Check gauge to assure proper fit.

SEE

Decreasing/Single Crochet, Seed and Double Seed
Patterns

FRONT

Bottom Rib: With smaller hook, ch 16.

Row 1: Sc in 2nd ch from hook and each ch across—
15 sts.

Rows 2–86 (94, 102): Ch 1, turn, sc in back lp only
of first st and each st across. Ch 1, work 86 (94, 102)
sc evenly spaced across long edge of rib. Change to
larger hook.

Body: **Row 1:** Ch 1, turn, sc in both lps of first st and
each st across.

Row 2: Ch 1, turn, sc in front lp only of first st and
each st across.

Row 3 (right side; seed pattern): Ch 1, turn, sc in
both lps of first st, sk next st current row, dc in unused
lp of sc 1 row below, *sc in both lps next st current
row, sk next st current row, dc in unused lp of sc 1
row below*, repeat * to * across.

Row 4: Repeat Row 2.

Row 5: Don't ch 1, turn, sk first st current row, dc in
unused lp of sc 1 row below, sc in both lps next st
current row, *sk next st current row, dc in unused lp
of sc 1 row below, sc in both lps next st current row*,
repeat * to * across.

Rows 6–9: Repeat Rows 2–5.

Rows 10–11: Repeat Row 1.

Row 12: Repeat Row 2.

Row 13 (double seed pattern): Ch 1, turn, sc in both
lps of first 2 sts, *(sk next st current row, dc in unused
lp of sc 1 row below)—2 times, (sc in both lps next st
current row)—2 times*, repeat * to * across.

Row 14: Repeat Row 2.

Row 15: Don't ch 1, turn, sk first 2 sts current row,
(dc in unused lp of sc 1 row below)—2 times, *(sc in
both lps next st current row)—2 times, (sk next st
current row, dc in unused lp of sc 1 row below)—2
times*, repeat * to * across.

Rows 16–19: Repeat Rows 12–15.

Rows 20–21: Repeat Row 1.

Repeat Rows 2–21 two times more, then Rows 2–11.

Neck Shaping: Work Row 2 across first 30 (34, 38) sts, sc 2 tog over next 2 sts (**dec made**); leave remaining sts unworked.

Decreasing 1 st at neck edge every row, work Rows 13–17.

Working even on 26 (30, 34) sts, repeat Rows 18–21, then 2–11 (13, 15).

Sizes Medium and Large Only: Repeat Row 1 one time.

All Sizes: Leaving center 22 sts free, shape opposite side of neck edge to correspond.

BACK

Work as for front through Body Row 1.

Repeat Row 1 until piece measures 20½″ (21″, 21½″) from beginning.

Neck Shaping: Ch 1, turn, sc across first 27 (31, 35) sts, sc 2 tog over next 2 sts (**dec made**); leave remaining sts unworked.

Continuing in sc, dec 1 st at neck edge every row 2 times.

Work even in sc on 26 (30, 34) sts until piece measures 22″ (22½″, 23″) from beginning.

Leaving center 28 sts free, shape opposite side of neck edge to correspond.

FINISHING

With right sides facing, sew front to back at shoulder seams.

Neckband: With right side facing and smaller hook, start at center back and work 101 (105, 109) sc evenly spaced around neck opening; join with sl st to first sc; end.

Rib: With smaller hook, ch 9.

Row 1: Sc in 2nd ch from hook and each ch across—8 sts.

Rows 2–101 (105, 109): Ch 1, turn, sc in back lp only of first st and each st across. Ch 1, work 101 (105, 109) sc evenly spaced across long edge of rib.

Starting at center back, with right sides facing, sew neckband to neck opening and short edges of neckband together.

Armhole Bands: On both front and back, mark st 7½″ (8″, 8½″) down from shoulder seam. With right side facing and smaller hook, work 71 (75, 79) sc evenly spaced between markers. Ch 1, turn, sc in first 2 (4, 6) sts, sc 2 tog, *sc in next 3 sts, sc 2 tog*, repeat * to * across, ending with sc in last 2 (4, 6) sts—57 (61, 65) sts; end.

Rib: Work as for neckband but for 57 (61, 65) rows. Ch 1, work 57 (61, 65) sc evenly spaced across long edge of rib.

Sew rib to armhole edge and sew side seam.

Repeat other side.

Secure and trim loose ends.

Tulip Vest

BEGINNER

*The rows of budding pastel tulips on this vest
herald the arrival of an early spring.*

SIZE

Small (Medium, Large)
Finished bust: 38″ (42″, 46″)
Back length: 21½″ (22″, 22½″)

MATERIALS

Brunswick Windmist (brushed, worsted weight Or-
lon acrylic), 1¾ oz/135 yd balls: 5 (6, 7) balls
Black (MC); 2 balls Green (A), 1 ball each Gold
(B) and Rose (C)
Size G crochet hook (or size for gauge)

GAUGE

18 sts = 4″; 10 rows = 4″ (in pattern st)
Check gauge to assure proper fit.

SEE

Changing Color/End of Row, Clusters, Decreasing/
Double Crochet, Reverse Slip Stitch, Surface Slip
Stitch, and Working with Chain Spaces/In

FRONT SIDE ONE

With MC, ch 45 (49, 53).

Row 1: Dc in 4th ch from hook and each ch across—
43 (47, 51) sts.

Rows 2–4: With MC, ch 3 (for first dc), turn, sk first
st, dc in each st across.

Row 5: With A, ch 3 (for first dc), turn, sk first 2 sts,
*dc in next st, ch 1, dc in **same** st, sk next st*, repeat
* to * across, ending with dc in last st.

Row 6: With B, ch 4 (for first dc, ch 1), turn, sk first
2 sts, *yo, insert hook into next ch 1 sp, yo, draw up
a lp, yo, draw through first 2 lps on hook, (yo, insert
hook into **same** ch 1 sp, yo, draw up a lp, yo, draw
through first 2 lps on hook)—2 times, yo, draw through
all 4 lps on hook—**cluster made**—ch 1, sk next 2 sts*,
repeat * to * across, ending with sk 1 st (rather than
2), dc in last st.

Row 7: With MC, ch 3 (for first dc), turn, sk first st,
dc in first ch 1 sp, *dc in top of next cluster, dc in
next ch 1 sp*, repeat * to * across, ending with dc in
last st.

Rows 8–11: Repeat Rows 2–5.

Row 12: With C, repeat Row 6.

Row 13: Repeat Row 7.

Repeat Rows 2–13 one time more, then Rows 2–7.

Armhole Shaping: Work Row 8 across first 35 (39, 43)
sts; leave remaining sts unworked.

Decreasing 1 st at armhole edge every row, work Rows
9–10.

Working even on 33 (37, 41) sts, repeat Rows 11–13,
then Rows 2–7; end.

Neck Shaping: Sk first 12 sts, rejoin yarn and work
Row 8 across.

Decreasing 1 st at neck edge every row, work Rows 9–
10.

Working even on 19 (23, 27) sts, repeat Rows 11–13, then Row 2 (2–3, 2–4).

FRONT SIDE TWO

Work as for Front Side One, reversing armhole and neck shaping.

BACK

With MC, ch 89 (97, 105).

Row 1: Dc in 4th ch from hook and each ch across— 87 (95, 103) sts.

Work Rows 2–13 of front on 87 (95, 103) sts.

Repeat Rows 2–13 one time more, then Rows 2–7; end.

Armhole Shaping: Sk first 8 sts, rejoin yarn and work Row 8 across next 71 (79, 87) sts; leave remaining sts unworked.

Decreasing 1 st each edge every row, work Rows 9– 10.

Working even on 67 (75, 83) sts, repeat Rows 11–13, then 2–13.

Sizes Medium and Large Only: Repeat Row 2 (2–3) one time more.

All Sizes: Neck Shaping: Work Row 2 (3, 4) across first 18 (22, 26) sts, dc 2 tog over next 2 sts; leave remaining sts unworked.

Leaving center 27 sts free, shape opposite side of neck edge to correspond.

FINISHING

With right sides facing, sew front panels to back at shoulder and side seams.

Edging: With right side facing and MC, start at side seam and work 1 rnd sc around entire garment edge (bottom, center front, and neckline), **working 3 sc at each corner;** join with sl st to first sc. Ch 1, don't turn, work 1 rnd reverse sl st into previous rnd; join with sl st to first reverse sl st. Ch 1, don't turn, working **below** previous rnd, work 1 rnd surface sl st around posts of first edging rnd; join with sl st to first surface sl st. Repeat the last rnd 1 time more; end.

Finish armhole openings in same manner.

Secure and trim loose ends.

Rosebud Pullover

ADVANCED

Capture the beauty of a summer garden with the rosebud clusters on this charming pullover.

SIZE

Small (Medium, Large)
Finished bust: 38" (43", 48")
Back length: 22½" (23", 23½")
Sleeve inseam: 19" (19½", 20")

MATERIALS

Reynolds Kitten (brushed, worsted weight acrylic and wool blend), 1¾ oz/160 yd balls: 8 (9, 10) balls White (MC); 1 ball each Green (A) and Mauve (B)
Size G crochet hook (or size for gauge)

GAUGE

27 sts = 7"; 19 rows = 9" (in pattern st)
Check gauge to assure proper fit.

SEE

Changing Color/End of Row and Within a Row, Clusters, Decreasing/Double Crochet, and Increasing

NOTE

Use a new strand of yarn for each motif; don't carry yarn.

FRONT

Bottom Rib: With MC, ch 16.

Row 1: With MC, sc in 2nd ch from hook and next 4 chs; with B, sc in next ch; with MC, sc in next ch; with A, sc in next ch; with MC, sc in next ch; with B, sc in next ch; with MC, sc in last 5 chs.

Rows 2–75 (85, 95): With MC, ch 1, turn, sc in back lp only of first 5 sts; with B, sc in back lp only of next st; with MC, sc in back lp only of next st; with A, sc in back lp only of next st; with MC, sc in back lp only of next st; with B, sc in back lp only of next st; with MC, sc in back lp only of last 5 sts. With MC, ch 1, work 75 (85, 95) sc evenly across long edge of rib.

Body: **Row 1:** With MC, ch 3 (for first dc), turn, sk first st, dc in each st across.

Row 2 (right side): With MC, ch 3 (for first dc), turn, sk first st, dc in next 4 sts, *sk next 2 sts; with A, dc in next st; (with MC, dc in **same** st; with A, dc in **same** st)—2 times, sk next 2 sts; with MC, dc in next 5 sts*, repeat * to * across.

Row 3: With MC, ch 3 (for first dc), turn, sk first st, dc in next 6 sts; [with B, yo, insert hook in next st, yo, draw up a lp, yo, draw through 2 lps, (yo, insert hook in **same** st, yo, draw up a lp, yo, draw through 2 lps)—2 times; with MC, yo, draw through all 4 lps on hook]—**dc cluster made; repeat [to] each time directions call for dc cluster;** *with MC, dc in next 9 sts; with B, dc cluster in next st*, repeat * to * across, ending with MC dc in in last 7 sts.

Rows 4–5: Repeat Row 1.

Row 6: With MC, ch 3 (for first dc), turn, sk first st, dc in next 9 sts, *sk next 2 sts; with A, dc in next st; (with MC, dc in **same** st; with A, dc in **same** st)—2 times, sk next 2 sts; with MC, dc in next 5 sts*, repeat * to * across, ending with MC dc in last 5 sts.

Row 7: With MC, ch 3 (for first dc), turn, sk first st, dc in next 11 sts; *with B, dc cluster in next st; with MC, dc in next 9 sts*, repeat * to * across, ending with MC dc in last 3 sts.

Rows 8–9: Repeat Row 1.

Repeat Rows 2–9 three times more.

Neck Shaping: Work Row 2 across first 25 (30, 35) sts; with MC, dc in next 2 sts, dc 2 tog over next 2 sts **(dec made)**; leave remaining sts unworked.

Next Row: With MC, ch 2, turn, sk first st **(dec made)**, dc in next 9 (4, 9) sts; *with B, dc cluster in next st; with MC, dc in next 9 sts*; *Sizes Medium and Large Only:* Repeat * to * 1 time more; *All Sizes:* With B, dc cluster in next st; with MC, dc in last 7 sts.

Decreasing 1 st at neck edge every row, repeat Rows 4–5.

Sizes Small and Large Only: Working even on 25 (35) sts, repeat Rows 6–7.

Size Medium Only: Working even on 30 sts, repeat Row 6 **but** omit MC dc in last 5 sts. Work next row as for Row 7 **but** begin with MC dc in first 7 sts (rather than 12).

All Sizes: Repeat Rows 8–9.

Size Medium Only: Repeat Row 1 one time more.

Size Large Only: Repeat Rows 2–3 one time more.

All Sizes: Leaving center 17 sts free, shape opposite side of neck edge to correspond.

BACK

Work as for front through Body Row 1.

With MC only, repeat Row 1 until piece measures 21½″ (22″, 22½″) from beginning.

Neck Shaping: Work Row 1 across first 24 (29, 34) sts, dc 2 tog over next 2 sts **(dec made)**; leave remaining sts unworked.

Work even in dc on 25 (30, 35) sts for 1 row.

Leaving center 23 sts free, shape opposite side of neck edge to correspond.

SLEEVES (make two)

Work rib as for front but for 31 (33, 35) rows. Ch 1, work 35 (37, 39) sc evenly spaced across long edge of rib.

Work Row 1 of front on 35 (37, 39) sts.

With MC only and continuing in dc, inc 1 st each edge next row and every other row 12 (13, 14) times.

Work even in dc on 61 (65, 69) sts until piece measures 19″ (19½″, 20″) from beginning.

FINISHING

With right sides facing, sew front to back at shoulder seams. Center sleeves at shoulder seams and sew together. Sew sleeve and side seams.

Neckband: With right side facing and MC, start at center back and work 81 (85, 89) sc evenly spaced around neck opening; join with sl st to first sc; end.

Rib: With MC, ch 8.

Row 1: With MC, sc in 2nd ch from hook; with B, sc in next ch; with MC, sc in next ch; with A, sc in next ch; with MC, sc in next ch; with B, sc in next ch; with MC, sc in last ch—7 sts.

Rows 2–81 (85, 89): With MC, ch 1, turn, sc in back lp only of first st; with B, sc in back lp only of next st; with MC, sc in back lp only of next st; with A, sc in back lp only of next st; with MC, sc in back lp only of next st; with B, sc in back lp only of next st; with MC, sc in back lp only of last st. With MC, ch 1, work 81 (85, 89) sc evenly spaced across long edge of rib.

With right sides facing, start at center back and sew neckband to neck opening and short edges of neckband together.

Secure and trim loose ends.

Combination Stitch Patterns

Pullover with Textured Border

BEGINNER

Bobbled borders add fashion flair to this stylish
but simple short-sleeved sweater.

SIZE

Small (Medium, Large)
Finished bust: 38″ (42″, 46″)
Back length: 21″ (21½″, 22″)
Sleeve inseam: 5″ (5½″, 6″)

MATERIALS

Patons Beehive Shetland Light (worsted weight
    acrylic and wool blend), 1¾ oz/145 yd balls:
    8 (9, 10) balls in color of choice
Sizes H and I crochet hooks (or size for gauge)

GAUGE

16 sts = 4″; 20 rows = 4″ (in pattern st)
Check gauge to assure proper fit.

SEE

Increasing, Reverse Slip Stitch, Surface Slip Stitch,
and Triple Crochet Bobbles

FRONT

With larger hook, ch 78 (86, 94).

Border: **Row 1:** Sc in 2nd ch from hook and each ch
across—77 (85, 93) sts.

Row 2 (wrong side): Ch 1, turn, sl st in first st, *tr in
next st, sl st in next st*, repeat * to * across (**tr bobbles
formed on right side**).

Row 3: Ch 1, turn, sc in first st and each st across.

Rows 4–17: Repeat Rows 2 and 3 (**border ends**).

Work even in sc on 77 (85, 93) sts until piece measures
13″ from beginning; end.

Armhole Shaping: Sk first 9 (10, 11) sts, rejoin yarn
and sc across next 59 (65, 71) sts; leave remaining sts
unworked.

Work even in sc on 59 (65, 71) sts, ending with right
side row, until piece measures 15″ (15½″, 16″) from
beginning.

Neck Border: Ch 1, turn, sc in first 10 (12, 14) sts,
sl st in next st, (tr in next st, sl st in next st)—19 (20,
21) times, sc in last 10 (12, 14) sts.

Next Row: Ch 1, turn, sc in first st and each st across.

Repeat the last 2 rows 3 times more.

Neck Shaping: Ch 1, turn, sc in first 10 (12, 14) sts,
sl st in next st, (tr in next st, sl st in next st)—4 times;
leave remaining sts unworked.

Next Row: Ch 1, turn, sc in first st and each st across.

Working even on 19 (21, 23) sts, repeat the last 2 rows,
ending with right side row, until piece measures 21″
(21½″, 22″) from beginning.

Leaving center 21 (23, 25) sts free, shape opposite side
of neck edge to correspond.

BACK

Work as for front through armhole shaping.

Work even in sc on 59 (65, 71) sts until piece measures
17½″ (18″, 18½″) from beginning.

Work neck border and neck shaping as for front.

SLEEVES (make two)

With larger hook, ch 54 (56, 58).

Rows 1–3: Work as for Rows 1–3 of front, but on 53 (55, 57) sts.

Row 4: Ch 1, turn, sc in first st, **sl st in same st (inc made),** tr in next st, *sl st in next st, tr in next st*, repeat * to * across, end with **sl st and sc in last st (inc made).**

Row 5: Repeat Row 3.

Row 6: Ch 1, turn, sl st in first 2 sts, *tr in next st, sl st in next st*, repeat * to * across, ending with sl st in last st.

Row 7: Increasing 1 st each edge, repeat Row 3.

Row 8: Repeat Row 2 **(border ends).**

Work even in sc on 57 (59, 61) sts for 2 rows.

Continuing in sc, inc 1 st each edge next row and every 3rd row 3 (4, 5) times.

Work even in sc on 65 (69, 73) sts until piece measures 7" (7½", 8") from beginning.

FINISHING

With right sides facing, sew front to back at shoulder seams, sleeves to sleeve openings, sleeve and side seams.

Edging: With right side facing and smaller hook, start at center back and work 1 rnd sc around neck opening; join with sl st to first sc. Ch 1, don't turn, work 1 rnd reverse sl st into previous rnd; join with sl st to first reverse sl st. Ch 1, don't turn, working **below** previous rnd, work 1 rnd surface sl st around posts of first edging rnd; join with sl st to first sl st; end.

Finish bottom and sleeve edges in same manner.

Secure and trim loose ends.

Textured Crewneck

BEGINNER

Bobbles abound on this pretty peach winter warmer.

SIZE

Small (Medium, Large)
Finished bust: 38″ (42″, 46″)
Back length: 22″ (22½″, 23″)
Sleeve inseam: 19½″ (20″, 20½″)

MATERIALS

Brunswick Windmist (brushed, worsted weight Orlon acrylic), 1¾ oz/135 yd balls: 11 (12, 13) balls in color of choice
Sizes I and J crochet hooks (or size for gauge)

GAUGE

15 sts = 4″; 18 rows = 4″ (in pattern st)
Check gauge to assure proper fit.

SEE

Decreasing/Single Crochet, Increasing, and Triple Crochet Bobbles

FRONT

Bottom Rib: With smaller hook, ch 14.

Row 1: Sc in 2nd ch from hook and each ch across—13 sts.

Rows 2–71 (79, 87): Ch 1, turn, sc in back lp only of first st and each st across. Ch 1, work 71 (79, 87) sc evenly spaced across long edge of rib. Change to larger hook.

Body: **Row 1 (wrong side):** Ch 1, turn, sl st in first st, *tr in next st, sl st in next st*, repeat * to * across **(tr bobbles formed on right side).**

Row 2: Ch 1, turn, sc in first st and each st across.

Row 3: Ch 1, turn, sl st in first 2 sts, *tr in next st, sl st in next st*, repeat * to * across, ending with sl st in last st.

Row 4: Repeat Row 2.

Repeat Rows 1–4, ending with Row 4, until piece measures 14″ from beginning; end.

Armhole Shaping: Sk first 8 sts; rejoin yarn and work Row 1 across next 55 (63, 71) sts.

Working even on 55 (63, 71) sts, repeat Rows 2–4, then Rows 1–4, ending with Row 4, until piece measures 18½″ from beginning.

Neck Shaping: Work Row 1 across first 21 (25, 29) sts; leave remaining sts unworked.

Next (Dec) Row: Ch 1, turn, sk first st **(dec made),** sc in next st and each st across.

Next Row: Work Row 3 across, **but** end with 1 sl st (rather than 2).

Next (Dec) Row: Repeat first decrease row.

Next Row: Repeat Row 1.

Next (Dec) Row: Repeat first decrease row.

Next Row: Work Row 3 across **but** end with 1 sl st (rather than 2).

Next (Dec) Row: Repeat first decrease row.

Working even on 17 (21, 25) sts, repeat Rows 1–4, ending with right side row, until piece measures 22″ (22½″, 23″) from beginning.

Leaving center 13 sts free, shape opposite side of neck edge to correspond.

BACK

Work as for front through ribbing.

Body: **Row 1:** Ch 1, turn, sc in first st and each st across.

Repeat Row 1 until piece measures 14″ from beginning; end.

Armhole Shaping: Sk first 8 sts, rejoin yarn and sc across next 55 (63, 71) sts; leave remaining sts unworked.

Work even in sc on 55 (63, 71) sts until piece measures 20½″ (21″, 21½″) from beginning.

Neck Shaping: Sc across first 20 (24, 28) sts; leave remaining sts unworked.

Continuing in sc, dec 1 st at neck edge next row and every other row 2 times.

Work even in sc on 17 (21, 25) sts until piece measures 22″ (22½″, 23″) from beginning.

Leaving center 15 sts free, shape opposite side of neck edge to correspond.

SLEEVES (make two)

Work rib as for front but for 30 (32, 34) rows. Ch 1, work 30 (32, 34) sc evenly spaced across long edge of rib. Change to larger hook.

Row 1: Ch 1, turn, sc in first 3 (4, 5) sts, 2 sc in next st **(inc made),** *sc in next 3 sts, 2 sc in next st **(inc made)***, repeat * to * across, ending with sc in last 2 (3, 4) sts—37 (39, 41) sts.

Rows 2–5: Ch 1, turn, sc in first st and each st across.

Continuing in sc, inc 1 st each edge next row and every 5th row 12 (13, 14) times.

Work even in sc on 63 (67, 71) sts until piece measures 21½″ (22″, 22½″) from beginning.

FINISHING

With right sides facing, sew front to back at shoulder seams, sleeves to sleeve openings, sleeve and side seams.

Neckband: With smaller hook, start at center back and work 70 (74, 78) sc evenly spaced around neck opening; join with sl st to first sc; end.

Rib: With smaller hook, ch 6.

Row 1: Sc in 2nd ch from hook and each ch across— 5 sts.

Rows 2–70 (74, 78): Ch 1, turn, sc in back lp only of first st and each st across. Ch 1, work 70 (74, 78) sc evenly spaced across long edge of rib.

Starting at center back, with right sides facing, sew neckband to neck opening and short edges of neckband together.

Secure and trim loose ends.

Country Cardigan

INTERMEDIATE

*The dusky shades of an autumn sunset were used
for this classic country cardigan.*

SIZE
Small (Medium, Large)
Finished bust: 38" (42", 46")
Back length: 23" (23½", 24")
Sleeve inseam: 19" (19½", 20")

MATERIALS
Brunswick Ballybrae (worsted weight unscoured
wool), 3½ oz/190 yd skeins: 6 (7, 7) skeins White
(MC), 1 skein each Blue Tweed (A) and Rose (B)
Sizes G and H crochet hooks (or size for gauge)
Ten ¾" buttons

GAUGE
21 sts = 6"; 10 rows = 4" (in pattern st)
Check gauge to assure proper fit.

SEE
Buttonholes, Changing Color/End of Row, Decreasing/Half Double Crochet, Increasing, and Triple
Crochet Bobbles

FRONT SIDE ONE

Bottom Rib: With MC and smaller hook, ch 14.

Row 1: Sc in 2nd ch from hook and each ch across—
13 sts.

Rows 2–33 (37, 41): Ch 1, turn, sc in back lp only
of first st and each st across. Ch 1, work 33 (37, 41)
sc evenly spaced across long edge of rib. Change to
larger hook.

Body: **Rows 1–2:** With MC, ch 2 (for first hdc), turn,
sk first st, hdc in each st across.

Row 3 (wrong side): With A, ch 1, turn, sl st in first
st, *tr in next st, sl st in next st*, repeat * to * across
(tr bobbles formed on right side).

Row 4: With MC, repeat Row 1.

Row 5: With B, repeat Row 1.

Row 6: With A, repeat Row 1.

Row 7: With MC, repeat Row 3.

Row 8: Repeat Row 6.

Row 9: Repeat Row 5.

Row 10: Repeat Row 4.

Row 11: Repeat Row 3.

Rows 12–21: Work as for Rows 2–11, **but use A when
B is called for and B when A is called for.**

Repeat Rows 2–21 one time more, then Rows 2–10.

Neck Shaping: Work Row 11 across first 27 (31, 35)
sts; leave remaining sts unworked.

Decreasing 1 st at neck edge every row, work Rows
12–15.

Working even on 23 (27, 31) sts, repeat Rows 16–19
(20, 21).

Size Large Only: Repeat Row 1 one time more.

FRONT SIDE TWO

Work as for Front Side One, reversing neck shaping.

BACK

Work rib as for front, but for 71 (79, 87) rows. Ch 1, work 71 (79, 87) sc evenly spaced across long edge of rib. Change to larger hook.

With MC only, work Body Row 1 of front on 71 (79, 87) sts.

Repeat Row 1 until piece measures 22" (22½", 23") from beginning.

Neck Shaping: Hdc across first 23 (27, 31) sts, hdc 2 tog over next 2 sts (**dec made**); leave remaining sts unworked.

Continuing in hdc, dec 1 st at neck edge next row.

Work even in hdc on 23 (27, 31) sts for 1 row.

Leaving center 21 sts free, shape opposite side of neck edge to correspond.

SLEEVES (make two)

Work rib as for front, but for 30 (32, 34) rows. Ch 1, work 37 (41, 45) sc evenly spaced across long edge of rib. Change to larger hook.

Rows 1–3: With MC only, work Body Row 1 of front on 37 (41, 45) sts.

Continuing in hdc, inc 1 st each edge next row and every 4th row 9 times.

Work even in hdc on 57 (61, 65) sts until piece measures 19" (19½", 20") from beginning.

FINISHING

With right sides facing, sew front panels to back at shoulder seams. Center sleeves at shoulder seams and sew together. Sew sleeve and side seams.

Collar: With right side facing, MC and smaller hook, begin at center front and work 78 (82, 86) sc evenly spaced around neck opening; end.

Rib: With MC and smaller hook, ch 19.

Row 1: Sc in 2nd ch from hook and each ch across— 18 sts.

Rows 2–78 (82, 86): Ch, 1 turn, sc in back lp only of first st and each st across. Ch 1, work 78 (82, 86) sc evenly spaced across long edge of rib.

With right side of both pieces up, start at center front and sew collar to neck opening.

Buttonhole Band: With MC and smaller hook, ch 7.

Row 1: Sc in 2nd ch from hook and each ch across— 6 sts.

Rows 2–3: Ch 1, turn, sc in back lp only of first st and each st across.

Row 4: Ch 1, turn, sc in back lp only of first 2 sts, ch 2, sk next 2 sts (**buttonhole made**), sc in back lp only of last 2 sts.

Row 5: Ch 1, turn, sc in back lp only of first 2 sts, 2 sc in ch 2 sp, sc in back lp only of last 2 sts.

Rows 6–12: Repeat Row 2.

Repeat Rows 4–12 eight times more, then Rows 4–7 (**10 buttonholes**).

With right sides facing, sew buttonhole band to inner edge of right front, beginning at lower edge of bottom rib and **ending ¾" above collar seam.**

Button Band: Work as for buttonhole band, **omitting buttonholes,** and sew to left front.

Finish buttonholes with buttonhole stitch and sew on buttons to correspond to buttonholes.

Secure and trim loose ends.

Pullover with Chevrons and Diamonds
INTERMEDIATE

*Flatter yourself with bobbled chevrons and diamonds
on a heathery blue sweater designed to
banish those midwinter blues.*

SIZE

Small (Medium, Large)
Finished bust: 38″ (42″, 46″)
Back length: 22″ (22½″, 23″)
Sleeve inseam: 10½″ (11″, 11½″)

MATERIALS

Bernat Berella "4" (worsted weight acrylic), 3½ oz/
    240 yd balls: 5 (6, 7) balls in color of choice
Sizes J and K crochet hooks (or size for gauge)

GAUGE

25 sts = 7″; 18 rows = 4″ (in pattern st)
Check gauge to assure proper fit.

SEE

Decreasing/Single Crochet, Increasing, and Triple
Crochet Bobbles

FRONT

Bottom Rib: With smaller hook, ch 16.

Row 1: Sc in 2nd ch from hook and each ch across—
15 sts.

Rows 2–67 (75, 83): Ch 1, turn, sc in back lp only
of first st and each st across. Ch 1, work 67 (75, 83)
sc evenly spaced across long edge of rib. Change to
larger hook.

Body: **Row 1 (wrong side):** Ch 1, turn, sl st in first
st, *tr in next st, sl st in next st*, repeat * to * across
(tr bobbles formed on right side).

Row 2: Ch 1, turn, sc in first st and each st across.

Row 3: Ch 1, turn, sc in first st, sl st in next st, *tr
in next st, sl st in next st*, repeat * to * across, ending
with sc in last st.

Row 4: Repeat Row 2.

Rows 5–12: Repeat Rows 1–4.

Row 13 (bobble chevrons begin): Ch 1, turn, sc in
first 2 sts, *sl st in next st, (tr in next st, sl st in next
st)—3 times, sc in next st*, repeat * to * across, ending
with sc in last st.

Row 14: Repeat Row 2.

Row 15: Ch 1, turn, sc in first 3 sts, *sl st in next st
(tr in next st, sl st in next st)—2 times, sc in next 3
sts*, repeat * to * across.

Row 16: Repeat Row 2.

Row 17: Ch 1, turn, sc in first 4 sts, sl st in next st,
tr in next st, sl st in next st, *sc in next 5 sts, sl st in
next st, tr in next st, sl st in next st*, repeat * to *
across, ending with sc in last 4 sts **(chevrons end).**

Rows 18–20: Repeat Row 2.

Row 21 (bobble diamonds begin): Ch 1, turn, sc in first 8 sts, *sl st in next st, tr in next st, sl st in next st, sc in next 5 sts*, repeat * to * across, ending with sc in last 3 sts.

Row 22: Repeat Row 2.

Row 23: Ch 1, turn, sc in first 7 sts, *sl st in next st, (tr in next st, sl st in next st)—2 times, sc in next 3 sts*, repeat * to * across, ending with sc in last 4 sts.

Row 24: Repeat Row 2.

Row 25: Repeat Row 21 (**diamonds end**).

Repeat Row 2 until piece measures 14″ from beginning; end.

Armhole Shaping: Sk first 3 sts, rejoin yarn and sc across next 61 (69, 77) sts; leave remaining sts unworked.

Continuing in sc, dec 1 st each edge next row and every other row 2 times.

Work even in sc on 55 (63, 71) sts until piece measures 19″ from beginning.

Neck Shaping: Ch 1, turn, sc across first 20 (24, 28) sts; leave remaining sts unworked.

Continuing in sc, dec 1 st at neck edge next row and every other row 2 times.

Work even in sc on 17 (21, 25) sts until piece measures 22″ (22½″, 23″) from beginning.

Leaving center 15 sts free, shape opposite side of neck edge to correspond.

BACK

Work as for front through ribbing.

Body: **Row 1:** Ch 1, turn, sc in first st and each st across.

Repeat Row 1 until piece measures 14″ from beginning.

Shape armholes as for front.

Work even in sc on 55 (63, 71) sts until piece measures 21″ (21½″, 22″) from beginning.

Neck Shaping: Ch 1, turn, sc across first 19 (23, 27) sts; leave remaining sts unworked.

Continuing in sc, dec 1 st at neck edge every row 2 times.

Work even in sc on 17 (21, 25) sts for 1 row.

Leaving center 17 sts free, shape opposite side of neck edge to correspond.

SLEEVES (make two)

Rib: With smaller hook, ch 11.

Row 1: Sc in 2nd ch from hook and each ch across—10 sts.

Rows 2–33 (35, 37): Ch 1, turn, sc in back lp only of first st and each st across. Ch 1, work 39 (41, 43) sc evenly spaced across long edge of rib. Change to larger hook.

Body: **Rows 1–2:** Ch 1, turn, sc in first st and each st across.

Row 3 (wrong side; bobble diamonds begin): Ch 1, turn, 2 sc in first st (**inc made**), sc in next 1 (2, 3) sts, sl st in next st, tr in next st, sl st in next st, *sc in next 5 sts, sl st in next st, tr in next st, sl st in next st*, repeat * to * across, ending with sc in next 1 (2, 3) sts, 2 sc in last st (**inc made**)—41 (43, 45) sts.

Row 4: Repeat Row 1.

Row 5: Ch 1, turn, sc in first 2 (3, 4) sts, sl st in next st, (tr in next st, sl st in next st)—2 times, *sc in next 3 sts, sl st in next st, (tr in next st, sl st in next st)—2 times*, repeat * to * across, ending with sc in last 2 (3, 4) sts.

Row 6: Increasing 1 st each edge, repeat Row 1—43 (45, 47) sts.

Row 7: Ch 1, turn, sc in first 4 (5, 6) sts, sl st in next st, tr in next st, sl st in next st, *sc in next 5 sts, sl st in next st, tr in next st, sl st in next st*, repeat * to * across, ending with sc in last 4 (5, 6) sts (**diamonds end**).

Row 8: Repeat Row 1.

Continuing in sc, inc 1 st each edge next row and every 3rd row 6 (7, 8) times.

Work even in sc on 57 (61, 65) sts until piece measures 10½" (11", 11½") from beginning; end.

Shape Cap: Sk first 3 sts, rejoin yarn and sc across next 51 (55, 59) sts; leave remaining sts unworked.

Continuing in sc, dec 1 st each edge next row and every other row 2 times—45 (49, 53) sts.

Continuing in sc, dec 1 st each edge every row until 15 sts remain.

FINISHING

With right sides facing, sew front to back at shoulder seams, sleeves to sleeve openings, sleeve and side seams.

Neckband: With smaller hook, start at center back and work 66 (70, 74) sc evenly spaced around neck opening; join with sl st to first sc; end.

Rib: With smaller hook, ch 6.

Row 1: Sc in 2nd ch from hook and each ch across— 5 sts.

Rows 2–66 (70, 74): Ch 1, turn, sc in back lp only of first st and each st across. Ch 1, work 66 (70, 74) sc evenly spaced across long edge of rib.

With right sides facing, start at center back and sew neckband to neck opening and short edges of neckband together.

Secure and trim loose ends.

Cardigans with Complementary Patterns and Ascending Diamonds

INTERMEDIATE

Two exquisite cardigans in icy-pale colors
to throw over your shoulders on a cool summer evening
or dress up a skirt with casual sophistication.

SIZE
Small (Medium, Large)
Finished bust: 38″ (42″, 46″)
Back length: 22″ (22″, 22½″)
Sleeve inseam: 19″ (19½″, 20″)

MATERIALS
Pingouin Le Yarn 3 (worsted weight acrylic, wool, and polypropylene blend), 3½ oz/200 yd balls: 6 (7, 8) balls/per sweater in color of choice
Sizes I and J crochet hooks (or size for gauge)
Eight ¾″ buttons

GAUGE
24 sts = 7″; 21 rows = 5″ (in pattern st)
Check gauge to assure proper fit.

SEE
Buttonholes, Decreasing/Single Crochet, Increasing, and Triple Crochet Bobbles

Complementary Patterns

FRONT SIDE ONE—STAGGERED DIAMONDS

Bottom Rib: With smaller hook, ch 14.

Row 1: Sc in 2nd ch from hook and each ch across—13 sts.

Rows 2–31 (35, 39): Ch 1, turn, sc in back lp only of first st and each st across. Ch 1, work 31 (39, 43) sc evenly spaced across long edge of rib. Change to larger hook.

Body: **Rows 1–2:** Ch 1, turn, sc in first st and each st across.

Row 3 (wrong side): Ch 1, turn, sc in first 6 (8, 6) sts, sl st in next st, tr in next st, sl st in next st, *sc in next 5 sts, sl st in next st, tr in next st, sl st in next st*, repeat * to * across, ending with sc in last 6 (8, 6) sts (**tr bobbles formed on right side of work**).

Row 4: Repeat Row 2.

Row 5: Ch 1, turn, sc in first 5 (7, 5) sts, sl st in next st, (tr in next st, sl st in next st)—2 times, *sc in next 3 sts, sl st in next st, (tr in next st, sl st in next st)—2 times*, repeat * to * across, ending with sc in last 5 (7, 5) sts.

Rows 6–7: Repeat Rows 2–3.

Rows 8–10: Repeat Row 2.

Row 11: Ch 1, turn, sc in first 2 (4, 2) sts, sl st in next st, tr in next st, sl st in next st, *sc in next 5 sts, sl st

in next st, tr in next st, sl st in next st*, repeat * to * across, ending with sc in last 2 (4, 2) sts.

Row 12: Repeat Row 2.

Row 13: Ch 1, turn, sc in first 1 (3, 1) sts, sl st in next st, (tr in next st, sl st in next st)—2 times, *sc in next 3 sts, sl st in next st, (tr in next st, sl st in next st)—2 times*, repeat * to * across, ending with sc in last 1 (3, 1) sts.

Rows 14–16: Repeat Rows 10–12.

Repeat Rows 1–16 three times more.

Neck Shaping: Work Row 1 across first 23 (27, 31) sts; leave remaining sts unworked.

Next (Dec) Row: Ch 1, turn, sk first st (**dec made**), sc in each st across.

Next (Dec) Row: Work as for Row 3 across, **but** end with sc in 3 (5, 3) sts, sc 2 tog over last 2 sts (**dec made**).

Next (Dec) Row: Repeat first decrease row.

Next (Dec) Row: Work as for Row 5 across, **but** end as follows: *Sizes Small and Large Only:* Sc 2 tog over last 2 sts; *Size Medium Only:* Sc in next 2 sts, sc 2 tog over last 2 sts.

All Sizes: Working even on 19 (23, 27) sts, repeat Row 2.

Next Row: Work as for Row 3 **but** end with sc in last 2 (4, 2) sts.

Work even in sc for 3 rows.

Next Row: Work as for Row 11 **but** end with sc in last 6 (8, 6) sts.

Next Row: Repeat Row 2.

Next Row: Work as for Row 13, **but** end with sc in last 5 (7, 5) sts.

Next Row: Repeat Row 2.

Next Row: Work as for Row 11, **but** end with sc in last 6 (8, 6) sts.

Work even in sc for 1 (1, 3) rows.

Closeup of details in Complementary Patterns sweater

FRONT SIDE TWO—STAGGERED BOBBLES

Work as for Front Side One through ribbing.

Body: **Rows 1–4:** Repeat Row 1 of Front Side One.

Row 5: Repeat Row 3 of Front Side One.

Rows 6–12: Repeat Row 1 of Front Side One.

Row 13: Repeat Row 11 of Front Side One.

Rows 14–20: Repeat Row 1 of Front Side One.

Repeat Rows 5–20 two times more, then rows 5–16; end.

Neck Shaping: Sk first 8 sts, rejoin yarn and sc across next 23 (27, 31) sts.

Continuing in sc, dec 1 st at neck edge every row 3 times.

Next (Dec) Row: Ch 1, turn, sk first st (**dec made**), sc in next 2 (4, 2) sts, sl st in next st, tr in next st, sl st in next st, (sc in next 5 sts, sl st in next st, tr in next st, sl st in next st)—1 (1, 2) times, end with sc in last 6 (8, 6) sts.

Work even in sc on 19 (23, 27) sts for 7 rows.

Next Row: Ch 1, turn, sc in first 6 (8, 6) sts, sl st in next st, tr in next st, sl st in next st, (sc in next 5 sts, sl st in next st, tr in next st, sl st in next st)—1 (1, 2) times, sc in last 2 (4, 2) sts.

Work even in sc for 3 (3, 5) rows.

Ascending Diamonds

FRONT SIDE ONE

Work as for Front Side One of Complementary Patterns through ribbing.

Body: **Row 1 (wrong side):** Ch 1, turn, sc in first 2 (4, 3) sts, sl st in next st, tr in next st, sl st in next st, *sc in next 5 (5, 7) sts, sl st in next st, tr in next st, sl st in next st*, repeat * to * across, ending with sc in last 2 (4, 3) sts (**tr bobbles formed on right side**).

Row 2: Ch 1, turn, sc in first st and each st across.

Row 3: Ch 1, turn, sc in first 1 (3, 2) sts, sl st in next st, (tr in next st, sl st in next st)—2 times, *sc in next 3 (3, 5) sts, sl st in next st, (tr in next st, sl st in next st)—2 times*, repeat * to * across, ending with sc in last 1 (3, 2) sts.

Row 4: Repeat Row 2.

Rows 5–6: Repeat Row 1–2.

Row 7: Ch 1, turn, sc in first 6 (8, 8) sts, sl st in next st, tr in next st, sl st in next st, *sc in next 5 (5, 7) sts, sl st in next st, tr in next st, sl st in next st*, repeat * to * across, ending with sc in last 6 (8, 8) sts.

Row 8: Repeat Row 2.

Row 9: Ch 1, turn, sc in first 5 (7, 7) sts, sl st in next st, (tr in next st, sl st in next st)—2 times, *sc in next 3 (3, 5) sts, sl st in next st, (tr in next st, sl st in next

st)—2 times*, repeat * to * across, ending with sc in last 5 (7, 7) sts.

Rows 10–12: Repeat Rows 6–8.

Repeat Rows 1–12 one time more.

Work even in sc for 6 rows, then repeat Rows 7–12 one time.

Repeat the last 12 rows 1 time more.

Work even in sc for 6 rows.

Next Row: Ch 1, turn, sc in first 14 (16, 18) sts, sl st in next st, tr in next st, sl st in next st, sc in last 14 (16, 18) sts.

Next Row: Work even in sc.

Next Row: Ch 1, turn, sc in first 13 (15, 17) sts, sl st in next st, (tr in next st, sl st in next st)—2 times, sc in last 13 (15, 17) sts.

Next Row: Work even in sc.

Next Row: Ch 1, turn, sc in first 14 (16, 18) sts, sl st in next st, tr in next st, sl st in next st, sc in last 14 (16, 18) sts (**pattern ends**).

Work even in sc until piece measures 18″ from beginning.

Neck Shaping: Ch 1, turn, sc across first 23 (27, 31) sts; leave remaining sts unworked.

Dec 1 st at neck edge every row 4 times.

Work even in sc on 19 (23, 27) sts until piece measures 22″ (22″, 22½″) from beginning.

FRONT SIDE TWO

Work as for Front Side One, reversing neck shaping.

BACK (both sweaters)

Work rib as for front, but for 67 (75, 83) rows. Ch 1, work 67 (75, 83) sc evenly spaced across long edge of rib. Change to larger hook.

Body: **Row 1:** Ch 1, turn, sc in first st and each st across.

Repeat Row 1 until piece measures 21¼″ (21¼″, 21¾″) from beginning.

Neck Shaping: Ch 1, turn, sc across first 21 (25, 29) sts; leave remaining sts unworked.

Continuing in sc, dec 1 st at neck edge every row 2 times—19 (23, 27) sts.

Leaving center 25 sts free, shape opposite side of neck edge to correspond.

SLEEVES (both sweaters; make two)

Rib: With smaller hook, ch 11.

Row 1: Sc in 2nd ch from hook and each ch across—10 sts.

Rows 2–26 (28, 30): Ch 1, turn, sc in back lp only of first st and each st across. Ch 1, work 38 (42, 46) sc evenly spaced across long edge of rib. Change to larger hook.

Body: **Rows 1–9:** Ch 1, turn, sc in first st and each st across.

Inc 1 st each edge next row and every 10th row 5 times.

Work even in sc on 50 (54, 58) sts until piece measures 19″ (19½″, 20″) from beginning.

FINISHING (both sweaters)

With right sides facing, sew front panels to back at shoulder seams. Center sleeves at shoulder seams and sew together. Sew sleeve and side seams.

Neckband: With smaller hook, ch 5.

Row 1: Sc in 2nd ch from hook and each ch across—4 sts.

Rows 2–76 (76, 80): Ch 1, turn, sc in back lp only of first st and each st across.

Starting at center front, with right sides facing, sew neckband to neck opening.

Buttonhole Band: With smaller hook, ch 7.

Row 1: Sc in 2nd ch from hook and each ch across—6 sts.

Rows 2–3: Ch 1, turn, sc in back lp only of first st and each st across.

Row 4: Ch 1, turn, sc in back lp only of first 2 sts, ch 2, sk 2 sts, sc in back lp only of last 2 sts (**buttonhole made**).

Row 5: Ch 1, turn, sc in back lp only of first 2 sts, 2 sc in ch 2 sp, sc in back lp only of last 2 sts.

Rows 6–11: Repeat Row 2.

Repeat Rows 4–11 six times more, then Rows 4–7—**eight buttonholes.**

With right sides facing, sew buttonhole band to inner edge of right front.

Button Band: Work as for buttonhole band, but **omit buttonholes** and sew to inner edge of left front.

Finish buttonholes with buttonhole stitch and sew on buttons to correspond to buttonholes.

Secure and trim loose ends.

Richly Textured Ski Sweater

INTERMEDIATE

A rich design of bobbles, moss, and seed patterns
texture this berry-colored crewneck.

SIZE

Small (Medium, Large)
Finished bust: 40″ (44″, 48″)
Back length: 24″ (24½″, 25″)
Sleeve inseam: 19″ (19½″, 20″)

MATERIALS

Patons Beehive Shetland Chunky (chunky weight
  acrylic and wool blend), 1¾ oz/82 yd balls: 15
  (18, 21) balls in choice of color
Sizes J and K crochet hooks (or size for gauge)

GAUGE

20 sts = 7″; 14 rows = 4″ (in pattern st)
Check gauge to assure proper fit.

SEE

Decreasing/Single Crochet, Increasing, Moss and
Seed Patterns, and Triple Crochet Bobbles

FRONT

Bottom Rib: With smaller hook, ch 11.

Row 1: Sc in 2nd ch from hook and each ch across—
10 sts.

Rows 2–57 (63, 69): Ch 1, turn, sc in back lp only
of first st and each st across. Ch 1, work 57 (63, 69)
sc evenly spaced across long edge of rib. Change to
larger hook.

Body: Row 1 (wrong side): Ch 1, turn, sc in front lp
only of first st and each st across.

Row 2 (seed pattern): Ch 1, turn, sc in both lps of
first st, *sk next st current row, dc in unused lp of sc
1 row below, sc in both lps next st current row*, repeat
* to * across.

Row 3: Repeat Row 1.

Row 4: Ch 1, turn, sk first st current row, dc in unused
lp of sc 1 row below, *sc in both lps next st current
row, sk next st current row, dc in unused lp of sc 1
row below*, repeat * to * across.

Rows 5–8: Repeat Rows 1–4.

Rows 9–10: Ch 1, turn, sc in both lps of first st and
each st across.

Row 11 (triple crochet bobbles): Ch 1, turn, sl st in
first st, *tr in next st, sl st in next st*, repeat * to *
across (**bobbles formed on right side**).

Rows 12–14: Repeat Row 9.

Row 15 (moss pattern): Ch 1, turn, sl st in first st,
hdc in next st, sl st in next st, repeat * to * across
(**texture pattern formed on right side**).

Row 16: Repeat Row 9.

Rows 17–22: Repeat Rows 15 and 16.

Rows 23–28: Repeat Rows 9–14.

Repeat Rows 1–18 one time more; end.

Armhole Shaping: Sk first 6 sts, rejoin yarn and work
Row 19 across next 45 (51, 57) sts; leave remaining
sts unworked.

Working even on 45 (51, 57) sts, repeat Rows 20–28, then Rows 1–8 (10, 12).

Neck Shaping: Work Row 9 (11, 13) across first 17 (19, 21) sts; leave remaining sts unworked.

Decreasing 1 st at neck edge every row, work Rows 10–13 (12–15, 14–17).

Working even on 13 (15, 17) sts, repeat Rows 14–18 (16–20, 18–22).

Leaving center 11 (13, 15) sts free, shape opposite side of neck edge to correspond.

BACK

Work as for front through ribbing.

Body: **Row 1:** Ch 1, turn, sc in both lps of first st and and each st across.

Repeat Row 1 until piece measures 16″ from beginning; end.

Armhole Shaping: Sk first 6 sts, rejoin yarn and sc across next 45 (51, 57) sts; leave remaining sts unworked.

Work even in sc on 45 (51, 57) sts until piece measures 23″ (23½″, 24″) from beginning.

Neck Shaping: Sc across first 15 (17, 19) sts; leave remaining sts unworked.

Continuing in sc, dec 1 st at neck edge every row 2 times.

Work even in sc on 13 (15, 17) sts for 1 row.

Leaving center 15 (17, 19) sts free, shape opposite side of neck edge to correspond.

SLEEVES (make two)

Work rib as for front but for 25 (27, 29) rows. Ch 1, work 25 (27, 29) sc evenly spaced across long edge of rib.

Row 1: Ch 1, turn, sc in first 4 (5, 6) sts, *2 sc in next st **(inc made)**, sc in next 4 sts*, repeat * to * across, ending with 2 sc in next st **(inc made)**, sc in last 5 (6, 7) sts—29 (31, 33) sts.

Rows 2–5: Ch 1, turn, sc in first st and each st across.

Continuing in sc, inc 1 st each edge next row and every 6th row 7 (8, 9) times.

Work even in sc on 45 (49, 53) sts until piece measures 21″ (21½″, 22″) from beginning.

FINISHING

With right sides facing, sew front to back at shoulder seams, sleeves to sleeve openings, sleeve and side seams.

Neckband: With right side facing and smaller hook, start at center back and work 54 (58, 62) sc evenly spaced around neck opening; join with sl st to first sc; end.

Rib: With smaller hook, ch 5.

Row 1: Sc in 2nd ch from hook and each ch across—4 sts.

Rows 2–54 (58, 62): Ch 1, turn, sc in back lp only of first st and each st across. Ch 1, work 54 (58, 62) sc evenly spaced across long edge of rib.

Starting at center back, with right sides facing, sew neckband to neck opening and short edges of neckband together.

Secure and trim loose ends.

Fisherman-style Pullover

ADVANCED

*Magnificent detail adds feminine appeal
to this traditional fisherman's sweater.*

SIZE

Small (Medium, Large)
Finished bust: 39″ (43″, 47″)
Back length: 21″ (21½″, 22″)
Sleeve inseam: 19″ (19½″, 20″)

MATERIALS

Bernat Berella "4" (worsted weight acrylic), 3½ oz/
   240 yd balls: 7 (8, 9) balls in color of choice
Sizes G, J, and K crochet hooks (or size for gauge)

GAUGE

27 sts = 7″; 17 rows = 4″ (in pattern st)
Check gauge to assure proper fit.

SEE

Cables, Decreasing/Single Crochet, Increasing, Seed
Pattern, Triple Crochet Bobbles, and Working
around Posts/Double Crochet Rib

NOTE

Garment is worked from side to side, rather than
from hem to shoulder

FRONT

With K hook, ch 72 (74, 76).

Row 1: Sc in 2nd ch from hook and each ch across—
71 (73, 75) sts.

Row 2—(seed pattern; wrong side): Ch 1, turn, sc in
front lp only of first st and each st across.

Row 3: Ch 1, turn, sc in both lps first st, *sk next st
current row, dc in unused lp of sc 1 row below, sc in
both lps next st current row*, repeat * to * across.

Row 4: Repeat Row 2.

Row 5: Ch 1, turn, sk first st current row, dc in unused
lp of sc 1 row below, *sc in both lps next st current
row, sk next st current row, dc in unused lp of sc 1
row below*, repeat * to * across.

Rows 6–19 (23, 27): Repeat Rows 2–5, ending with
Row 3 **(seed pattern ends)**.

Rows 20–21 (24–25, 28–29): Ch 1, turn, sc in both
lps of first st and each st across.

**Row 22 (26,30)—(triple crochet bobbles formed on
right side)**: Ch 1, turn, sl st in first st, *tr in next st,
sl st in next st*, repeat * to * across **(bobbles end)**.

Rows 23–24 (27–28, 31–32): Repeat Row 20 (24, 28).

Row 25 (29, 33)—(cable pattern): Ch 1, turn, sc in
first st, *ch 3, sk next 2 sts, sc in next st, **turn,** sc in
each of the 3 chs just completed, sl st in sc **(cable
made), turn,** working **behind** cable, work 1 sc in first
sk st, then 2 sc in last sk st*, repeat * to * across. *Sizes
Small and Large Only:* End with sc in last 1 (2) sts
(cable pattern ends). *All Sizes:* **Rows 26–27 (30–31,
34–35)**: Repeat Row 20 (24, 28).

**Row 28 (32, 36)—(triple crochet bobbles formed on
right side)**: Repeat Row 22 (26, 30) **(bobbles end)**.
Change to size J hook.

Rows 29–31 (33–35, 37–39): Repeat Row 20 (24, 28).

Neck Shaping: **Row 32 (36, 40):** Ch 1, turn, sc in both lps of first 64 sts; leave remaining sts unworked.

Rows 33–35 (37–39, 41–43): Continuing in sc, dec 1 st at neck edge every row—61 sts.

Row 36 (40, 44)—(bobble diamond pattern; triple crochet bobbles formed on right side): Ch 1, turn, sc in first 4 sts, sl st in next st, tr in next st, sl st in next st, *sc in next 7 sts, sl st in next st, tr in next st, sl st in next st*, repeat * to * across, ending with sc in last 4 sts.

Row 37 (41, 45): Ch 1, turn, sc in both lps of first st and each st across.

Row 38 (42, 46): Ch 1, turn, sc in first 3 sts, sl st in next st, (tr in next st, sl st in next st)—2 times, *sc in next 5 sts, sl st in next st, (tr in next st, sl st in next st)—2 times*, repeat * to * across, ending with sc in last 3 sts.

Row 39 (43, 47): Repeat Row 37 (41, 45).

Row 40 (44, 48): Repeat Row 36 (40, 44).

Rows 41–43 (45–47, 49–51): Repeat Row 37 (41, 45).

Row 44 (48, 52): Ch 1, turn, sc in first 9 sts, sl st in next st, tr in next st, sl st in next st, *sc in next 7 sts, sl st in next st, tr in next st, sl st in next st*, repeat * to * across, ending with sc in last 9 sts.

Row 45 (49, 53): Repeat Row 37 (41, 45).

Row 46 (50, 54): Ch 1, turn, sc in first 8 sts, sl st in next st, (tr in next st, sl st in next st)—2 times, *sc in next 5 sts, sl st in next st, (tr in next st, sl st in next st)—2 times*, repeat * to * across, ending with sc in last 8 sts.

Row 47 (51, 55): Repeat Row 37 (41, 45).

Row 48 (52, 56): Repeat Row 44 (48, 52).

Repeat Row 37 (41, 45) 3 times, then Rows 36–40 (40–44, 44–48) **(bobble diamond pattern ends).**

Working in sc, inc 1 st at neck edge every row 3 times.

Work even in sc on 64 sts for 1 row.

Next Row: Ch 8 (10, 12), turn, sc in 2nd ch from hook, in each new ch and each st across.

Work even in sc on 71 (73, 75) sts for 2 rows. *Change to size K hook.*

Repeat Rows 22–28 (26–32, 30–36) 1 time, Row 20 (24, 28) 3 times, then Rows 2–19 (23, 27) 1 time.

BACK

Work as for front through Row 5.

Repeat Rows 2–5 six (seven, eight) times more.

Neck Shaping: Repeat Row 2, ending with sc 2 tog **(dec made).**

Decreasing 1 st at neck edge every row, repeat Rows 3–5.

Working even on 67 (69, 71) sts, repeat Rows 2–5 four times, then Rows 2–3.

Increasing 1 st at neck edge every row, repeat Rows 4–5, then Rows 2–3.

Working even on 71 (73, 75) sts, repeat Rows 4–5, then Rows 2–5 six (seven, eight) times, then Rows 2–3.

SLEEVES (make two)

With K hook, ch 36 (38, 40).

Row 1: Sc in 2nd ch from hook and each ch across— 35 (37, 39) sts.

Rows 2–5: Work Rows 2–5 of front on 35 (37, 39) sts.

Row 6 (Inc): Increasing 1 st each edge, repeat Row 2.

Row 7: Repeat Row 5.

Rows 8–9: Repeat Rows 2–3.

Row 10 (Inc): Repeat Row 6—39 (41, 43) sts.

Repeat Rows 3–10 five (six, six) times more.

Sizes Small and Large Only: Repeat Rows 3–7 one time more.

All Sizes: Working even on 61 (65, 69) sts, repeat Rows 2–5, ending with right side row, until piece measures 17″ (17½″, 18″) from beginning.

FINISHING

Bottom Rib: With right side facing and J hook, work 86 (94, 102) sc evenly spaced across lower edge of front. *Change to size G hook.*

Row 1: Ch 3 (for first dc), turn, sk first st, dc in each st across.

Row 2: Ch 1, turn, fpdc around first st, bpdc around next st, *fpdc around next st, bpdc around next st*, repeat * to * across.

Rows 3–7: Repeat Row 2.

Work back rib as for front.

Cuff: With right side facing and J hook, work 34 (36, 38) sc evenly spaced across lower edge of sleeve. *Change to size G hook.*

Work Rows 1–4 of bottom rib.

Repeat on other sleeve.

With right sides facing, sew front to back at shoulder seams. Center sleeves at shoulder seams and sew together. Sew sleeve and side seams.

Neckband: With right side facing and J hook, work 70 (74, 78) sc evenly spaced around neck opening; join with sl st to first sc. *Change to size G hook.*

Work Row 1 of bottom rib around; join with sl st to first dc.

Work Row 2 of bottom rib around; join with sl st to first fpdc; end.

Secure and trim loose ends.

Fair Isle–style Turtleneck
BEGINNER

*Wherever you go, you'll travel in style wearing
this beautifully patterned, luxuriously soft turtleneck.*

SIZE
Small (Medium, Large)
Finished bust: 38" (42", 46")
Back length: 22" (22½", 23")
Sleeve inseam: 19" (19½", 20")

MATERIALS
Pingouin Mousse (brushed, worsted weight acrylic),
   1¾ oz/155 yd balls: 7 (8, 9) balls Burgundy (MC);
   1 (1, 2) balls Cream (A); and 1 ball Rose (B)
Size H crochet hook (or size for gauge)

GAUGE:
16 sts = 4"; 12 rows = 5" (in pattern st)
Check gauge to assure proper fit.

SEE
Changing Color/End of Row, Decreasing/Double
Crochet, Increasing, and Working around Posts/
Front

FRONT

Bottom Rib: With MC, ch 14.

Row 1: Sc in 2nd ch from hook and each ch across—
13 sts.

Rows 2–75 (83, 91): Ch 1, turn, sc in back lp only
of first st and each st across. Ch 1, work 75 (83, 91)
sc evenly spaced across long edge of rib.

Body: **Row 1:** With MC, ch 3 (for first dc), turn, sk
first st, dc in each st across.

Row 2: With A, repeat Row 1.

Row 3: With B, repeat Row 1.

Row 4 (right side): With A, ch 3 (for first dc), turn,
sk first st, *sk next st current row, working in **front** of
previous row, tr **around post** of dc **below** next st, dc
in next st current row*, repeat * to * across.

Row 5: With MC, repeat Row 1.

Row 6: With B, repeat Row 1.

Repeat Rows 1–6 five times more, then repeat Row 1
one time.

Neck Shaping: Work Row 2 across first 30 (34, 38)
sts; leave remaining sts unworked.

Decreasing 1 st at neck edge next row and every other
row 2 times, work Rows 3–6, then Row 1.

Working even on 27 (31, 35) sts, repeat Rows 2–5.

Sizes Medium and Large Only: Repeat Row 1 one
(two) times more.

All Sizes: Leaving center 15 sts free, shape opposite
side of neck edge to correspond.

BACK

Work as for front through Body Row 1.

With MC only, repeat Row 1 until piece measures
20½" (21", 21½") from beginning.

Neck Shaping: Ch 3 (for first dc), turn, sk first st, dc across next 27 (31, 35) sts; leave remaining sts unworked.

Continuing in dc, dec 1 st at neck edge next row.

Work even in dc on 27 (31, 35) sts for 1 row.

Leaving center 19 sts free, shape opposite side of neck edge to correspond.

SLEEVE (make two)

Work rib as for front but for 30 (32, 34) rows. Ch 1, work 30 (32, 34) sc evenly spaced across long edge of rib.

Row 1: With MC only, ch 3 (for first dc), turn, sk first st, dc in next 2 (3, 4) sts, 2 dc in next st **(inc made)**, *dc in next 3 sts, 2 dc in next st **(inc made)***, repeat * to * across, ending with dc in last 2 (3, 4) sts—37 (39, 41) sts.

Row 2: Ch 3 (for first dc), turn, sk first st, dc in each st across.

Continuing in dc, inc 1 st each edge next row and every other row 11 (12, 13) times.

Work even in dc on 61 (65, 69) sts until piece measures 19″ (19½″, 20″) from beginning.

FINISHING

With right sides facing, sew front to back at shoulder seams. Center sleeves at shoulder seams and sew together. Sew sleeve and side seams.

Collar: With MC, start at center back and work 82 (86, 90) sc evenly spaced around neck opening; join with sl st to first sc; end.

Rib: With MC, ch 32.

Row 1: Sc in 2nd ch from hook and each ch across—31 sts.

Rows 2–82 (86, 90): Ch 1, turn, sc in back lp only of first st and each st across. Ch 1, work 82 (86, 90) sc evenly spaced across long edge of rib.

Sew short edges of collar together to form tube.

With tube and sweater right side out, insert tube in neck opening, start at center back and sew together.

Secure and trim loose ends.

Rainbow Boatneck

BEGINNER

*Soft lilac, mauve, and pink add a rainbow of color
to this soft white boatneck.*

SIZE
Small (Medium, Large)
Finished bust: 42" (46", 50")
Back length: 26" (26", 26½")
Sleeve inseam: 21½" (22", 22½")

MATERIALS
Reynolds Kitten (brushed, worsted weight acrylic
and wool blend), 1¾ oz/160 yd balls: 8 (9, 9)
balls White (MC); 1 (2, 2) balls Lilac (A); 1 ball
each Mauve (B) and Pink (C)
Size H crochet hook (or size for gauge)

GAUGE
29 sts = 7"; 10 rows = 4" (in pattern st)
Check gauge to assure proper fit.

SEE
Changing Color/End of Row, Increasing, and
Working with Chain Spaces/Behind

FRONT/BACK (make two)

Bottom Rib: With MC, ch 11.

Row 1: Sc in 2nd ch from hook and each ch across—
10 sts.

Rows 2–87 (95, 103): Ch 1, turn, sc in back lp only
of first st and each st across. Ch 1, work 87 (95, 103)
sc evenly spaced across long edge of rib.

Body: **Row 1:** With MC, ch 3 (for first dc), turn, sk
first st, dc in next st and in each st across.

Row 2: With MC, ch 4 (for first dc, ch 1), turn, sk
first 2 sts, dc in next st, *ch 1, sk next st, dc in next
st*, repeat * to * across.

Row 3 (right side): With A, ch 3 (for first dc), turn,
sk first st, *sk next st current row, working **behind** next
ch 1 of previous row, tr into top of next sk st of that
row, dc in next st current row*, repeat * to * across.

Row 4: With A, repeat Row 2.

Rows 5–6: With MC, repeat Rows 3 and 2.

Rows 7–8: With B, repeat Rows 3 and 2.

Rows 9–10: With MC, repeat Rows 3 and 2.

Rows 11–12: With C, repeat Rows 3 and 2.

Row 13: With MC, repeat Row 3.

Repeat Rows 2–13 two times more.

Armhole Shaping: Sk first 10 sts, rejoin MC and work
Row 2 across next 67 (75, 83) sts; leave remaining sts
unworked.

Working even on 67 (75, 83) sts, repeat Rows 3–13,
then 2–5.

Size Large Only: With MC, repeat Row 1.

All Sizes: With MC, ch 1, turn, sc in first st and each
st across; end.

Neck Rib: Work as for Bottom Rib, but for 67 (75,
83) rows. Ch 1, turn, work 67 (75, 83) sc evenly spaced
across long edge of rib; end.

With right sides facing, sew long edge of neckband to top edge of front/back.

SLEEVES (make two)

Work rib as for front/back but for 30 (32, 34) rows. Ch 1, work 30 (32, 34) sc evenly spaced across long edge of rib.

Row 1: With MC only, ch 3 (for first dc), turn, sk first st, dc in next 2 (3, 4) sts, 2 dc in next st (**inc made**), *dc in next 3 sts, 2 dc in next st (**inc made**)*, repeat * to * across, ending with dc in last 2 (3, 4) sts—37 (39, 41) sts.

Row 2: Ch 3 (for first dc), turn, sk first st, dc in each st across.

Continuing in dc, inc 1 st each edge next row and every other row 15 (15, 16) times more—69 (71, 75) sts.

Work even in dc on 69 (71, 75) sts until piece measures 21½″ (22″, 22½″) from beginning.

FINISHING

On top of neckband, mark st 3½″ (4¼″, 5″) in from armhole edge, on each side of both front and back. With right sides facing, sew shoulder seams to markers. Sew sleeves to sleeve openings, sleeve and side seams.

Secure and trim loose ends.

Sunrise Jacket

INTERMEDIATE

The warm hues of a summer sunrise make this intricately patterned jacket a splendid addition to any wardrobe.

SIZE
Small (Medium, Large)
Finished bust: 38″ (42″, 46″)
Back length: 21½″ (22″, 22½″)
Sleeve inseam: 17½″ (18″, 18½″)

MATERIALS
Patons Cotton Sahara (terry, worsted weight cotton and nylon blend), 1¾ oz/115 yd balls: 11 (12, 13) balls Pink (MC); 2 balls each White (A) and Peach (B)
Sizes F and G crochet hooks (or size for gauge)

GAUGE
13 sts = 3″; 15 rows = 3″ (in pattern stitch)
Check gauge to assure proper fit.

SEE
Changing Color/End of Row, Decreasing/Single Crochet, Increasing, Reverse Slip Stitch, Spike Stitch, Surface Slip Stitch, Triple Crochet Bobbles, and Working with Chain Spaces/Behind

NOTE
For stitch counts, include each sc **and** each ch 1 sp

FRONT SIDE ONE

With MC and larger hook, ch 42 (46, 50).

Row 1: Sc in 2nd ch from hook and each ch across—41 (45, 49) sts.

Row 2: With A, ch 1, turn, sc in first st and each st across.

Rows 3–5: With B, repeat Row 2.

Row 6: With MC, ch 1, turn, sc in first st, *ch 1, sk next st, sc in next st*, repeat * to * across.

Row 7 (right side): With B, ch 1, turn, sc in first st, working **behind** ch 1 of previous row, sc in first sk st of that row, sc in next st, *working **behind** ch of 1 previous row, sc in next sk st of that row, sc in next st*, repeat * to * across.

Row 8: With A, ch 1, turn, sl st in first st, *tr in next st, sl st in next st*, repeat * to * across (**tr bobbles formed on right side**).

Row 9: With B, ch 1, turn, sc into space **below** first st (into same place that st was worked)—**spike sc made**—*sc in next st, spike sc in next st*, repeat * to * across.

Rows 10–11: Repeat Rows 6–7.

Rows 12–13: Repeat Rows 3–4.

Row 14: Repeat Row 2.

Rows 15–17: With MC, repeat Row 2.

Rows 18–33: Work as for Rows 2–17 **but use B when A is called for and A when B is called for.**

Repeat Rows 2–32 one time more.

Armhole Shaping: Work Row 33 across first 37 (41, 45) sts; leave remaining sts unworked.

Decreasing 1 st at armhole edge every row, work Rows 2–5.

Working even on 33 (37, 41) sts, repeat Rows 6–29.

Neck Shaping: Work Row 30 across first 25 (29, 33) sts; leave remaining sts unworked.

Decreasing 1 st at neck edge every row, work Rows 31–33, then Rows 2–4.

Working even on 19 (23, 27) sts, repeat Rows 5–13 (15, 17).

FRONT SIDE TWO

Work as for Front Side One, reversing armhole and neck shaping.

BACK

With MC, ch 82 (90, 98).

Row 1: Sc in 2nd ch from hook and each ch across— 81 (89, 97) sts.

Row 2: Ch 1, turn, sc in first st and each st across.

With MC only, repeat Row 2 until piece measures 13″ from beginning; end.

Armhole Shaping: Sk first 4 sts, rejoin yarn, sc across next 73 (81, 89) sts; leave remaining sts unworked.

Continuing in sc, dec 1 st each edge every row 4 times.

Work even in sc on 65 (73, 81) sts until piece measures 20¼″ (20¾″, 21¼″) from beginning.

Neck Shaping: Sc across first 22 (26, 30) sts; leave remaining sts unworked.

Continuing in sc, dec 1 st at neck edge every row 3 times.

Work even in sc on 19 (23, 27) sts until piece measures 21½″ (22″, 22½″) from beginning.

Leaving center 21 sts free, shape opposite side of neck edge to correspond.

SLEEVES (make two)

With MC, ch 39 (43, 47).

Row 1: Sc in 2nd ch from hook and each ch across— 38 (42, 46) sts.

Rows 2–3: Ch 1, turn, sc in first st and each st across.

Continuing with MC only and in sc, inc 1 st each edge next row and every 4th row 17 times.

Work even in sc on 74 (78, 82) sts until piece measures 17½″ (18″, 18½″) from beginning; end.

Shape Cap: Sk first 4 sts, rejoin yarn, sc across next 66 (70, 74) sts; leave remaining sts unworked.

Continuing in sc, dec 1 st each edge every row until 16 sts remain.

FINISHING

With right sides facing, sew front panels to back at shoulder seams, sleeves to sleeve openings, sleeve and side seams.

Edging: With right side facing, MC and smaller hook, start at side seam and work 1 rnd sc around entire garment edge (bottom, center front, and neckline), **working 3 sc at each corner;** join with sl st to first sc. Ch 1, don't turn, work 1 rnd reverse sl st into previous rnd; join with sl st to first reverse sl st. Ch 1, don't turn, working **below** previous rnd, work 1 rnd surface sl st around posts of first edging rnd; join with sl st to first sl st. Repeat the last rnd 1 time more; end.

Finish sleeve edges in same manner.

Secure and trim loose ends.

Cardigan with Vertical Stripes

ADVANCED

*Bold black stripes and buttons provide a dramatic contrast
to the brilliant fuchsia of this dressy cardigan.*

SIZE
Small (Medium, Large)
Finished bust: 38″ (42″, 46″)
Back length: 21½″ (22″, 22½″)
Sleeve inseam: 19″ (19½″, 20″)

MATERIALS:
Reynolds Kitten (brushed, worsted weight acrylic
    and wool blend), 1¾ oz/160 yd balls: 8 (9, 10)
    balls Fuchsia (MC); 1 ball Black (CC)
Ten ⁹⁄₁₆″ buttons
Size G crochet hook (or size for gauge)

GAUGE:
23 sts = 6″; 11 rows = 5″ (in pattern st)
Check gauge to assure proper fit.

SEE
Buttonholes, Changing Color/End of Row,
Decreasing/Double Crochet, Increasing, Spike
Stitch, Triple Crochet Bobbles, and Working with
Chain Spaces/In

NOTE
Garment is worked from side to side, rather than
from hem to shoulder

FRONT SIDE ONE

With MC, ch 73 (75, 77).

First Row: Dc in 4th ch from hook and each ch
across—71 (73, 75) sts.

Next Row: With MC, ch 3 (for first dc), turn, sk first
st, dc in each st across.

Repeat the last row 7 (9, 11) times more.

Stripe Pattern: **Row 1:** With CC, ch 4 (for first dc,
ch 1), turn, sk first 2 sts, dc in next st, *ch 1, sk next
st, dc in next st*, repeat * to * across.

Row 2 (right side): With MC, ch 3 (for first dc), turn,
sk first st, *sk next st current row, working **behind** next
ch 1 of previous row, tr into top of next sk st of that
row, dc in next st current row*, repeat * to * across.

Row 3: With MC, ch 1, turn, sc in first st and each
st across.

Row 4: With CC, ch 2 (for first hdc), turn, sk first st,
hdc in each st across.

Row 5: With MC, ch 1, turn, sl st in first st, *tr in
next st, sl st in next st*, repeat * to * across (**tr bobbles
formed on right side**).

Row 6: With CC, ch 1, turn, hdc into space **below**
first st (into same place that st was worked—**spike hdc
made**), *hdc in next st, spike hdc in next st*, repeat
* to * across.

Rows 7–8: Repeat Row 3.

Rows 9–10: Repeat Rows 1–2 (**stripe pattern ends**).

With MC only, work even in dc for 1 row.

Neck Shaping: Ch 3 (for first dc), turn, sk first st, dc
in next 58 sts, dc 2 tog over next 2 sts (**dec made**);
leave remaining sts unworked—60 sts.

Continuing in dc, dec 1 st at neck edge every row 2 times—58 sts; end.

Bottom Edging: With right side facing, work 39 (43, 47) sc evenly spaced across lower edge of front panel; end.

Rib: Ch 16.

Row 1: Sc in 2nd ch from hook and each ch across—15 sts.

Rows 2–39 (43, 47): Ch 1, turn, sc in back lp only of first st and each st across. Ch 1, work 39 (43, 47) sc evenly spaced across long edge of rib.

With right sides facing, sew rib to bottom edge of front panel.

FRONT SIDE TWO

Work as for Front Side One to neck shaping; end.

Neck Shaping: Sk first 10 (12, 14) sts, rejoin MC in next st, ch 2 **(dec made),** dc in next st and in each st across—60 sts.

Complete as for Front Side One.

BACK

Work as for Front Side One to stripe pattern.

With MC only, work even in dc for 7 more rows.

Neck Shaping: Ch 3 (for first dc), turn, sk first st, dc across next 63 (65, 67) sts, dc 2 tog over next 2 sts **(dec made);** leave remaining sts unworked.

Continuing in dc, dec 1 st at neck edge next row.

Work even in dc on 64 (66, 68) sts for 6 rows.

Continuing in dc, inc 1 st at neck edge every row 2 times—66 (68, 70) sts.

Next Row: Ch 3 (for first dc), turn, sk first st, dc in each st across; at end of row, with a separate strand of yarn, ch 5; dc in each new ch.

Work even in dc on 71 (73, 75) sts for 15 (17, 19) rows; end.

Bottom Edging: With right side facing, work 84 (92, 100) sc evenly spaced across lower edge of back; end. Work rib as for front panel but for 84 (92, 100) rows. Ch 1, work 84 (92, 100) sc evenly spaced across long edge of rib.

With right sides facing, sew rib to bottom edge of back.

SLEEVES (make two)

With right sides facing, sew front panels to back at shoulder seams.

Row 1: With right side facing, count 30 (32, 34) sts down from shoulder seam, join MC, ch 3 (for first dc), dc in next 29 (31, 33) sts, dc in shoulder joining, dc in next 30 (32, 34) sts—61 (65, 69) sts.

Rows 2–11 (10, 9): With MC only, ch 3 (for first dc), sk first st, dc in each st across.

Continuing in dc, dec 1 st each edge next row and every other row 11 (12, 13) times—37 (39, 41) sts.

Work even in dc for 1 row.

Next Row: Ch 1, turn, sc in first 3 (4, 5) sts, sc 2 tog **(dec made),** *sc in next 3 sts, sc 2 tog **(dec made)**,* repeat * to * across, ending with sc in last 2 (3, 4) sts—30 (32, 34) sts; end.

Rib: Work rib as for front panel but for 30 (32, 34) rows. Ch 1, work 30 (32, 34) sc evenly spaced across long edge of rib.

With right sides facing, sew rib to lower edge of sleeve.

Repeat other side.

FINISHING

Neckband: With right side facing and MC, start at center front and work 62 (66, 70) sc evenly spaced around neck opening; end.

Rib: With MC, ch 7.

Row 1: Sc in 2nd ch from hook and each ch across—6 sts.

Rows 2–62 (66,70): Ch 1, turn, sc in back lp only of first st and each st across. Ch 1, work 62 (66, 70) sc evenly spaced across long edge of rib.

With right sides facing, start at center front and sew neckband to neck opening. Sew sleeve and side seams.

Buttonhole Band: **Row 1:** With right side facing and MC, work 81 sc evenly spaced along entire inner edge (bottom rib, body, and neckband) of right front.

Rows 2–3: Ch 1, turn, sc in back lp only of first st and each st across.

Row 4: Ch 1, turn, sc in back lp only of first 4 sts, ch 1, sk next st **(buttonhole made)**, *sc in back lp only of next 7 sts, ch 1, sk next st **(buttonhole made)***, repeat * to * across, ending with sc in back lp only of last 4 sts—**10 buttonholes.**

Row 5: Ch 1, turn, sc in back lp only of first 4 sts, sc in ch 1 sp, *sc in back lp only of next 7 sts, sc in ch 1 sp*, repeat * to * across, ending with sc back lp only of last 4 sts.

Rows 6–7: Repeat Row 2.

Button Band: Work into left front, as for buttonhole band, **omitting buttonholes.**

Finish buttonholes with buttonhole stitch and sew on buttons to correspond to buttonholes.

Secure and trim loose ends.

Starry Pullover

INTERMEDIATE

Illuminate your summer evenings
with this delightful short-sleeved shell.

SIZE
Small (Medium, Large)
Finished bust: 38″ (42″, 46″)
Back length: 22″ (22½″, 23″)

MATERIALS
Unger Fluffy (brushed, worsted weight acrylic),
1¾ oz/156 yd balls: 6 (7, 8) balls in color of
choice
Sizes G, I, and J crochet hooks (or size for gauge)

GAUGE
11 sts = 3″; 13 rows = 3″ (in pattern st)
Check gauge to assure proper fit.

SEE
Decreasing/Single Crochet, Increasing, Star Stitch,
Surface Slip Stitch, and Working around Posts/
Double Crochet Rib

NOTE
Garment is worked from side to side, rather than
from hem to shoulder

FRONT

With size J hook, ch 30 (32, 34).

Row 1: Sc in 2nd ch from hook and each ch across—
29 (31, 33) sts.

Row 2: Ch 1, turn, sc in first st and each st across.
Repeat the last row 7 times more.

Sleeve Shaping: Ch 45, turn, sc in 2nd ch from hook,
in each new ch and each st across.

Work even in sc on 73 (75, 77) sts for 16 (20, 24)
rows.

Next Row (star stitch; right side): Ch 3, turn, insert
hook into 2nd ch from hook, yo, draw a lp through
ch, **keeping all lps on hook until star st is completed,**
insert hook into **next** ch, yo, draw a lp through ch,
insert hook into **first** st, yo, draw a lp through, (insert
hook into **next** st, yo, draw a lp through)—2 times,
yo, draw through all 6 lps on hook (star st made), ch
1, *insert hook under **last** ch 1, yo, draw a lp through,
keeping all lps on hook until star st is completed,
insert hook under both strands of **last** lp of **last** star,
yo, draw a lp through, insert hook into **same** st as for
last lp of last star, yo, draw a lp through, (insert hook
into **next** st, yo, draw a lp through)—2 times, **yo, draw
through all 6 lps on hook (star st made), ch 1***, repeat
* to * across, ending with sc in **same** st as for last lp
of final star.

Next Row: Ch 1, turn, sc in first st, *sc under next
ch 1 of last row, sc under both strands of next star st
lp*, repeat * to * across—73 (75, 77) sts.

Repeat the last 2 rows 1 time more.

Work even in sc for 3 rows.

Neck Shaping: Ch 1, turn, sc across first 62 sts; leave
remaining sts unworked.

Continuing in sc, dec 1 st at neck edge every row 3 times.

Work even in sc on 59 sts for 1 row.

Repeat the 2 rows of star st pattern above 6 times.

Working in sc, inc 1 st at neck edge every row 3 times.

Work even in sc on 62 sts for 1 row.

Next Row: Ch 12 (14, 16), turn, sc in 2nd ch from hook, in each new ch and each st across.

Work even in sc on 73 (75, 77) sts for 3 rows.

Repeat the 2 rows of star st pattern above 2 times.

Work even in sc for 16 (20, 24) rows.

Sleeve Shaping: Sc across first 29 (31, 33) sts; leave remaining sts unworked.

Work even in sc on 29 (31, 33) sts for 8 rows; end.

Surface Slip Stitch Star Panel Border: Border is worked **between** stitches with surface slip stitch. Yarn is held at back of work throughout. It is important that stitch tension be neither too tight nor too loose, and that a sufficient length of yarn be left at each end to secure later.

With right side facing and size I hook, begin the first border row as follows: Insert hook in space between first and second sts of row **preceding** first star st row of first star st side panel, holding yarn at back of work, yo, draw up a lp; *insert hook in sp directly beside st just worked, yo, draw up a lp and draw that lp through the lp on hook*, repeat * to * across.

Work the next border row, in the same manner, around posts of row **following** final star st row of the panel.

Repeat for center panel and remaining side panel.

BACK

Work as for front through sleeve shaping.

Work even in sc on 73 (75, 77) sts for 25 (29, 33) rows.

Neck Shaping: Ch 1, turn, sc across first 70 (72, 74) sts; leave remaining sts unworked.

Continuing in sc, dec 1 st at neck edge every row 3 times.

Work even in sc on 67 (69, 71) sts for 25 rows.

Continuing in sc, inc 1 st at neck edge every row 3 times. Work even in sc on 70 (72, 74) sts for 1 row.

Next Row: Ch 4, turn, sc in 2nd ch from hook, in each new ch and each st across.

Work even in sc on 73 (75, 77) sts for 25 (29, 33) rows.

Shape and work remaining sleeve as for front.

FINISHING

Bottom Rib: With right side facing and G hook, work 69 (77, 85) sc evenly spaced across lower edge of front.

Row 1: Ch 3 (for first dc), turn, sk first st, dc in each st across.

Row 2: Ch 1, turn, fpdc around first st, *bpdc around next st, fpdc around next st*, repeat * to * across.

Row 3: Ch 1, turn, bpdc around first st, *fpdc around next st, bpdc around next st*, repeat * to * across.

Row 4: Repeat Row 2.

Work back rib as for front.

With right sides facing, sew front to back at shoulder and side seams.

Neckband: With right side facing and G hook, start at center back and work 90 (94, 98) sc evenly spaced around neck opening; join with sl st to first sc. Work Row 1 of bottom rib around; join with sl st to first dc. Work Row 2 of bottom rib around; join with sl st to first fpdc; end.

Armhole Band: With right side facing and G hook, start at side seam and work 44 (48, 52) sc evenly spaced around sleeve edge; join with sl st st to first sc. Work rib as for neckband.

Repeat other side.

Secure and trim loose ends.

Tunisian Crochet

Pullover with Basketweave or Ridged Stripe Pattern

INTERMEDIATE

*Textured, or exploding with fireworks
of colorful stripes, a crewneck sweater
offers a multitude of fashion alternatives.*

SIZE
Small (Medium, Large)
Finished bust: 38" (42", 46")
Back length: 22" (22½", 23")
Sleeve inseam: 19" (19½", 20")

MATERIALS

Basketweave
Patons Valencia (brushed, sport weight acrylic
   and nylon blend), 1¾ oz/188 yd balls: 8 (10, 11)
   balls in color of choice

Ridged Stripes
Patons Valencia (see above): 8 (10, 11) balls White
   (MC); 1 ball each Blue (A), Teal (B), and Hot
   Pink (C)

Both Sweaters
14" afghan hooks, sizes H/8 and J/10; 22" flexible
   afghan hook, size H/8 (or size for gauge)
Size F crochet hook

GAUGE
19 sts = 4"; 17 rows = 4" (in pattern st)
Check gauge to assure proper fit.

SEE
Tunisian Crochet

Basketweave

FRONT

Bottom Rib: With H/14" afghan hook, ch 90 (100, 110).

Foundation Row: 1st half: Insert hook in 2nd ch from hook, yo, draw a lp through ch, *insert hook in next ch, yo, draw a lp through ch*, repeat * to * across, keeping all lps on hook for first half of all rows—90 (100, 110) lps on hook.

2nd half: Yo, draw through 1 lp, *yo, draw through 2 lps*, repeat * to * across. Row is complete. Always count lp remaining on hook as first st of next row.

Row 1: 1st half: Holding yarn in back of work, sk first vertical lp below, insert hook from **front to back** through center of next vertical lp (hook should pass under ch formed by 2nd half of previous row), yo, draw a lp through (knit stitch made; repeat this sequence each time instructions call for k), k1, holding yarn in front of work, insert hook from **back to front** through center of next vertical lp (hook should pass under ch formed by 2nd half of previous row), yo, draw a lp through (purl stitch made; repeat this sequence each time instructions call for p), *k3, p1*, repeat * to * across, ending with k2 (4, 2).

Closeup of details in Pullover with Basketweave

2nd half: Work 2nd half of all rows as for foundation row.

Rows 2–10: Repeat Row 1. Change to J/14″ hook.

NOTE: Stitch counts include lp remaining on hook at end of previous row as first knit stitch of current row.

Body: **Row 1:** K31 (36, 41), p4, (k4, p4)—3 times, k31 (36, 41).

Rows 2–4: Repeat Row 1.

Row 5: K35 (40, 45), p4, (k4, p4)—2 times, k35 (40, 45).

Rows 6–8: Repeat Row 5.

Repeat Rows 1–8 seven times more, then Rows 1–4.

Neck Shaping: K30 (35, 40); leave remaining sts unworked.

Next Row: K26 (31, 36), insert hook through center of next 2 vertical lps **simultaneously** (as for k), yo, draw through both lps (k2 tog made, repeat this sequence each time instructions call for k2 tog or dec of 1), k2.

Next Row: Knit.

In the same manner, dec 1 st at neck edge next row and every other row 1 time.

Knit even on 27 (32, 37) sts for 10 (12, 14) rows.

End as follows: Leaving a sufficient length of yarn to secure later, cut yarn; draw yarn end through lp remaining on hook.

Leaving center 30 sts free, shape opposite side of neck edge to correspond.

Ridged Stripes

FRONT

With MC, work as for Basketweave through ribbing. Change to J/14″ hook.

NOTE: Stitch counts include lp remaining on hook at end of previous row as first knit stitch of current row.

Body: **Rows 1–5:** With MC, knit.

Row 6: With A, knit.

Row 7: With A, k1, p88 (98, 108), k1.

Rows 8–13: With MC, knit.

Rows 14–15: With B, repeat Rows 6–7.

Rows 16–21: Repeat Rows 8–13.

Rows 22–23: With C, repeat Rows 6–7.

Rows 24–29: Repeat Rows 8–13.

Repeat Rows 6–29 one time more, then Rows 6–18.

Neck Shaping: Work Row 19 across first 30 (35, 40) sts; leave remaining sts unworked.

Next Row: Work Row 20 across first 26 (31, 36) sts, insert hook through center of next 2 vertical lps simultaneously (as for k), yo, draw through both lps (k2 tog made, repeat this sequence each time instructions call for k2 tog or dec of 1), k2.

Next Row: Repeat Row 21.

In the same manner, decreasing 1 st at neck edge next row and every other row 1 time, work Rows 22–24.

Working even on 27 (32, 37) sts, repeat Rows 25–29, then Rows 6–10 (12, 13).

Size Large Only: Repeat Row 13 one time more.

All Sizes: End as follows: Leaving a sufficient length of yarn to secure later, cut yarn; draw yarn end through lp remaining on hook.

Leaving center 30 sts free, shape opposite side of neck edge to correspond.

BACK (both sweaters)

Work as for front through ribbing.

Body: **Row 1:** With MC only, knit.

Repeat Row 1 until piece measures 20″ (20½″, 21″) from beginning.

Neck Shaping: K30 (35, 40); leave remaining sts unworked.

Work decrease rows as for front neckline.

Knit even on 27 (32, 37) sts for 3 rows.

Leaving center 30 sts free, shape opposite side of neck edge to correspond.

SLEEVES (both sweaters; make two)

Rib: With MC and H/14″ afghan hook ch 40 (43, 46). Work foundation row as for front.

Rows 1–10: K1 (3, 3), p1, *k3, p1*, repeat * to * across, ending with k2 (3, 2). Change to J/14″ hook.

Body: **Row 1:** K5 (3, 3), insert hook in space **between** st just worked and next vertical lp (hook should pass under ch formed by 2nd half of previous row), yo, draw up a lp (increase made; repeat this sequence each time instructions call for inc 1), *k4, inc 1*, repeat * to * across, ending with k3 (4, 3)—49 (53, 57) sts.

Rows 2–5: Knit.

Row 6: K1, inc 1, k47 (51, 55), inc 1, k1.

Rows 7–11: Knit.

In the same manner, inc 1 st each edge next row and every 6th row 10 times.

Knit even on 73 (77, 81) sts until piece measures 19″ (19½″, 20″) from beginning.

FINISHING (both sweaters)

With right sides facing, using standard crochet hook and MC, join front to back at shoulder seams with sl st, matching stitches and inserting hook through centers of vertical lps (as for k) but from wrong side of work. Center sleeves at shoulder seams and join together in the same manner. Join sleeve and side seams.

NOTE: Pick up stitches from an edge by inserting hook through center of vertical lp (as for k), yo, draw up a lp.

Neckband: With right side facing, MC and flexible afghan hook, begin at center back and pick up 110 (114,118) lps evenly spaced around neck opening. Work off in usual manner.

Rib: **Rows 1–5:** *K3, p1*, repeat * to * around, ending with k2; end.

With right sides facing, standard crochet hook, MC and sl st, join short edges of neckband together.

Edging: With standard crochet hook and MC, begin at center back of neckband by inserting hook through center of vertical lp (as for k), yo, draw a lp through, *insert hook through center of next vertical lp, yo, draw a lp through that lp **and** through lp on hook*, repeat * to * around.

End as follows: Leaving a sufficient length of yarn to secure later, cut yarn; insert hook into first st of edging rnd, yo, draw yarn end through to right side of work (weave back through to wrong side with tapestry needle before securing).

Work edging around cuffs and bottom rib in same manner.

Secure and trim loose ends.

Pullover with Bobble Chevrons

ADVANCED

*A delicate pullover that's always
in style — just change accessories
to suit your mood and the occasion.*

SIZE
Small (Medium, Large)
Finished bust: 38″ (42″, 46″)
Back length: 22½″ (23″, 23½″)
Sleeve inseam: 3″

MATERIALS
Phildar Prognostic (sport weight acrylic and wool
   blend), 1¾ oz/175 yd balls: 7 (8, 9) balls in color
   of choice
14″ afghan hooks, sizes H/8 and J/10; 22″ flexible
   afghan hook, size H/8 (or size for gauge)
Size F crochet hook

GAUGE
20 sts = 4″; 14 rows = 3″ (in pattern st)
Check gauge to assure proper fit.

SEE
Tunisian Crochet

FRONT

Bottom Rib: With H/14″ afghan hook, ch 96 (106, 116).

Foundation Row: *1st half:* Insert hook in 2nd ch from hook, yo, draw a lp through ch, *insert hook in next ch, yo, draw a lp through ch*, repeat * to * across, keeping all lps on hook for first half of all rows—96 (106, 116) lps on hook.

2nd half: Yo, draw through 1 lp, *yo, draw through 2 lps*, repeat* to * across. Row is complete. Always count lp remaining on hook as first stitch of next row.

Row 1: *1st half:* Holding yarn in back of work, sk first vertical lp below, insert hook from **front to back** through center of next vertical lp (hook should pass under ch formed by 2nd half of previous row), yo, draw a lp through (knit stitch made; repeat this sequence each time instructions call for k), k1, holding yarn in front of work, insert hook from **back to front** through center of next vertical lp (hook should pass under ch formed by 2nd half of previous row), yo, draw a lp through (purl stitch made; repeat this sequence each time instructions call for p), *k3, p1*, repeat * to * across, ending with k4 (2, 4).

2nd half: Work 2nd half of all rows as for foundation row.

Rows 2–10: Repeat Row 1. Change to J/14″ hook.

NOTE: Stitch counts include lp remaining on hook at end of previous row as first knit stitch of current row.

Body: **Rows 1–3:** Knit.

Row 4: K45 (50, 55), yo, insert hook from front to back through center of next vertical lp (as for k), yo,

draw a lp through, yo, draw through 2 lps, (yo, insert hook through center of **same** vertical lp, yo, draw a lp through, yo, draw through 2 lps)—3 times, yo, draw through 4 lps, yo, draw through 1 lp (bobble made; repeat this sequence each time instructions call for bobble), k4, bobble, k45 (50, 55).

Row 5: Knit.

Row 6: K43 (48, 53), bobble, k8, bobble, k43 (48, 53).

Row 7: Knit.

Row 8: K41 (46, 51), bobble, k12, bobble, k41 (46, 51).

Row 9: Knit.

Row 10: K39 (44, 49), bobble, k16, bobble, k39 (44, 49).

Row 11: Knit.

Row 12: K37 (42, 47), bobble, k20, bobble, k37 (42, 47).

Rows 13–14: Knit.

Repeat Rows 4–14 six times more; **and at the same time, when piece measures 14″ from beginning, shape sleeves as follows:** At end of 2nd half of row, ch 10; draw up a lp through each new ch (in same manner as for foundation row); work across row in pattern; at end of row with a separate strand of yarn, ch 10; draw up a lp through each new ch—116 (126, 136) lps on hook. Work the additional stitches on subsequent rows, maintaining established pattern.

Neck Shaping: K45 (50, 55); leave remaining sts unworked.

Next Row: K41 (46, 51), insert hook through center of next 2 vertical lps **simultaneously** (as for k), yo, draw through both lps (k2 tog made, repeat this sequence each time instructions call for k2 tog or dec of 1), k2.

Next Row: Knit.

In the same manner, dec 1 st at neck edge next row and every other row 1 time.

Knit even on 42 (47, 52) sts for 10 (12, 14) rows.

End as follows: Leaving a sufficient length of yarn to secure later, cut yarn; draw yarn end through lp remaining on hook.

Leaving center 26 sts free, shape opposite side of neck edge to correspond.

BACK

Work as for front through ribbing.

Body: **Row 1:** Knit.

Repeat Row 1 until piece measures 14″ from beginning.

Shape sleeves as for front.

Knit even on 116 (126, 136) sts until piece measures 20⅝″ (21⅛″, 21⅝″) from beginning.

Neck shaping: K44 (49, 54); leave remaining sts unworked.

Next Row: K40 (45, 50), k2 tog, k2.

Next Row: Knit.

In the same manner, dec 1 st at neck edge next row.

Knit even on 42 (47, 52) sts for 5 rows.

Leaving center 28 sts free, shape opposite side of neck edge to correspond.

FINISHING

With right sides facing and standard crochet hook, join front to back at shoulder seams with sl st, matching stitches and inserting hook through centers of vertical lps (as for k) but from wrong side of work.

NOTE: Pick up stitches from an edge by inserting hook through center of vertical lp (as for k), yo, draw up a lp.

Neckband: With right side facing and flexible afghan hook, begin at center back and pick up 106 (110, 114) lps evenly spaced around neck opening. Work off in usual manner.

Rib: **Rows 1–5:** *K3, p1*, repeat * to * around, ending with k2; end.

With right sides facing, standard crochet hook and sl st, join short edges of neckband together.

Cuff: With right side facing and H/14″ afghan hook, pick up 82 (86, 90) lps evenly spaced at sleeve edge. Work off in usual manner.

Rib: **Row 1:** *K1, k2 tog, k1, p1, k2 tog, k1, k2 tog, p1*, repeat * to * across; *Size Small Only:* End with (k2 tog)—2 times, k1—59 sts; *Size Medium Only:* End with k1, k2 tog, k1, p1, k2 tog, k2—63 sts; *Size Large Only:* End with (k1, k2 tog, k1, p1)—2 times, k3—67 sts.

All Sizes: **Rows 2–5:** *K3, p1*, repeat * to * across, ending with k3.

Repeat on other sleeve edge.

With right sides facing, standard crochet hook and sl st, join side seams.

Edging: With standard crochet hook, begin at center back of neckband by inserting hook through center of vertical lp (as for k), yo, draw a lp through, *insert hook through center of next vertical lp, yo, draw a lp through that lp **and** through lp on hook*, repeat * to * around.

End as follows: Leaving a sufficient length of yarn to secure later, cut yarn; insert hook into first st of edging rnd, yo, draw yarn end through to right side of work (weave back through to wrong side with tapestry needle before securing).

Work edging around cuffs and bottom rib in same manner.

Secure and trim loose ends.

Pullover with Waves

ADVANCED

You can almost smell the ocean breezes in the sea-blue waves of this distinctively patterned sweater.

SIZE
Small (Medium, Large)
Finished bust: 38″ (43″, 47″)
Back length: 22″ (22½″, 23″)

MATERIALS
Brunswick Cotton Candy (bouclé, worsted weight Orlon, cotton, nylon, and Lycra blend), 1¾ oz/110 yd balls: 8 (9, 10) balls White (MC); 1 ball each Teal (A) and Turquoise (B)
14″ afghan hooks, sizes H/8 and J/10; 22″ flexible afghan hook, size H/8 (or size for gauge)
Size F crochet hook
Knitting bobbins

GAUGE
36 sts = 7″; 36 rows = 7″ (in pattern st)
Check gauge to assure proper fit.

SEE
Tunisian Crochet

FRONT

Bottom Rib: With MC and H/14″ afghan hook, ch 97 (109, 121).

Foundation Row: *1st half:* Insert hook in 2nd ch from hook, yo, draw a lp through ch, *insert hook in next ch, yo, draw a lp through ch*, repeat * to * across, keeping all lps on hook for first half of all rows—97 (109, 121) lps on hook.

2nd half: Yo, draw through 1 lp, *yo, draw through 2 lps*, repeat * to * across. Row is complete. Always count lp remaining on hook as first stitch of next row.

Row 1: *1st half:* Holding yarn in back of work, sk first vertical lp below, insert hook from **front to back** through center of next vertical lp (hook should pass under ch formed by 2nd half of previous row), yo, draw a lp through (knit stitch made; repeat this sequence each time instructions call for k), holding yarn in front of work, insert hook from **back to front** through center of next vertical lp (hook should pass under ch formed by 2nd half of previous row), yo, draw a lp through (purl stitch made; repeat this sequence each time instructions call for p), *k3, p1*, repeat * to * across, ending with k2.

2nd half: Work 2nd half of all rows as for foundation row.

Rows 2–10: Repeat Row 1. Change to J/14″ hook.

NOTE: *Stitch counts include lp remaining on hook at end of previous row as first knit stitch of current row.*

Body: Rows 1–2: With MC, knit.

Next Row (see diagram): Work Row 1 of chart as follows: With A, knit.

Work Rows 2–6 of chart in same manner.

Work Row 7 of chart as follows: A to B: With A, k1; B to C: *With MC, k2; with B, k7; with MC, k2; with A, k1*, repeat * to * across—**Row 7 of chart completed.**

All Sizes

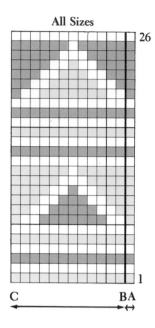

26

1

C BA

Each block represents one stitch and one row in Tunisian crochet knit

Work A to B one time, then repeat B to C across

Closeup of details in Pullover with Waves

In the same manner, work Rows 8–26 of chart.

Repeat Rows 1–26 of chart 1 time more, then Rows 1–5.

With MC only, work even in knit stitch until piece measures 14″ from beginning; end as follows: Leaving a sufficient length of yarn to secure later, cut yarn; draw yarn end through lp remaining on hook.

Armhole Shaping: Skip first 8 sts, rejoin MC and knit across next 81 (93, 105) sts; leave remaining sts unworked.

Next Row: K2, insert hook through center of next 2 vertical lps **simultaneously** (as for k), yo, draw through both lps (k2 tog made, repeat this sequence each time instructions call for k2 tog or dec of 1), k73 (85, 97), k2 tog, k2.

Next Row: Knit.

In the same manner, dec 1 st each edge next row and every other row 2 times.

Knit even on 73 (85, 97) sts until piece measures 18″ from beginning.

Neck Shaping: Knit across first 23 (29, 35) sts; leave remaining sts unworked.

Working decreases in same manner as for armholes, dec 1 st at neck edge next row and every other row 2 times.

Knit even on 20 (26, 32) sts until piece measures 22″ (22½″, 23″) from beginning; end.

Leaving center 27 sts free, shape opposite side of neck edge to correspond.

BACK

With MC only, work as for front through armhole shaping.

Knit even on 73 (85, 97) sts until piece measures 20½" (21", 21½") from beginning.

Shape neckline as for front.

FINISHING

With right sides facing, using standard crochet hook and MC, join front to back at shoulder and side seams with sl st, matching stitches and inserting hook through centers of vertical lps (as for k) but from wrong side of work.

NOTE: Pick up stitches from an edge by inserting hook through center of vertical lp (as for k), yo, draw up a lp.

Neckband: With right side facing, MC and flexible afghan hook, begin at center back and pick up 111 (115, 119) lps evenly spaced around neck opening. Work off in usual manner.

Rib: Rows 1–5: *K3, p1*, repeat * to * around, ending with k3; end.

With right sides facing, standard crochet hook, MC and sl st, join short edges of neckband together.

Armhole Bands: With right side facing, MC and flexible afghan hook, begin at side seam and pick up 94 (98, 102) lps evenly spaced around armhole opening. Work off in usual manner.

Rib: Rows 1–5: *K3, p1*, repeat * to * around, ending with k2.

With right sides facing, standard crochet hook, MC and sl st, join short edges of armhole band together.

Repeat on other armhole opening.

Edging: With standard crochet hook and MC, begin at center back of neckband by inserting hook through center of vertical lp (as for k), yo, draw a lp through, *insert hook through center of next vertical lp, yo, draw a lp through that lp **and** through lp on hook*, repeat * to * around.

End as follows: Leaving a sufficient length of yarn to secure later, cut yarn; insert hook into first st of edging rnd, yo, draw yarn end through to right side of work (weave back through to wrong side with tapestry needle before securing).

Work edging around armhole bands and bottom rib in same manner.

Secure and trim loose ends.

Pullover with Tulips

ADVANCED

*Delicate pink tulips blossom
on a uniquely feminine sweater.*

SIZE
Small (Medium, Large)
Finished bust: 38″ (42″, 46″)
Sleeve inseam: 9″
Back length: 22″ (22½″, 23″)

MATERIALS
Brunswick Cotton Candy (bouclé, worsted weight
Orlon, cotton, nylon, and Lycra blend), 1¾ oz/
110 yd balls: 11 (12, 14) balls Teal (MC); 1 ball
each White (A) and Mauve (B)
14″ afghan hooks, sizes H/8 and J/10; 22″ flexible afghan hook, size H/8 (or size for gauge)
Size F crochet hook
Knitting bobbins

GAUGE
20 sts = 4″; 24 rows = 5″ (in pattern st)
Check gauge to assure proper fit.

SEE
Tunisian Crochet

FRONT

Bottom Rib: With MC and H/14″ afghan hook, ch
95 (105, 115).

Foundation Row: *1st half:* Insert hook in 2nd ch from
hook, yo, draw a lp through ch, *insert hook in next
ch, yo, draw a lp through ch*, repeat * to * across,
keeping all lps on hook for first half of all rows—95
(105, 115) lps on hook.

2nd half: Yo, draw through 1 lp, *yo, draw through
2 lps*, repeat * to * across. Row is complete. Always
count lp remaining on hook as first stitch of next row.

Row 1: *1st half:* Holding yarn in back of work, sk first
vertical lp below, insert hook from **front to back**
through center of next vertical lp (hook should pass
under ch formed by 2nd half of previous row), yo,
draw a lp through (knit stitch made; repeat this sequence each time instructions call for k), k1, holding
yarn in front of work, insert hook from **back to front**
through center of next vertical lp (hook should pass
under ch formed by 2nd half of previous row), yo,
draw a lp through (purl stitch made; repeat this sequence each time instructions call for p), *k3, p1*,
repeat * to * across, ending with k3 (1, 3).

2nd half: Work 2nd half of all rows as for foundation
row.

Rows 2–15: Repeat Row 1. Change to J/14″ hook.

*NOTE: Stitch counts include lp remaining on hook at
end of previous row as first knit stitch of current row.*

Body: Row 1: With MC, knit.

Repeat Row 1 until piece measures 12½″ from
beginning.

Next Row (see diagram): With MC, k10 (10, 12); work

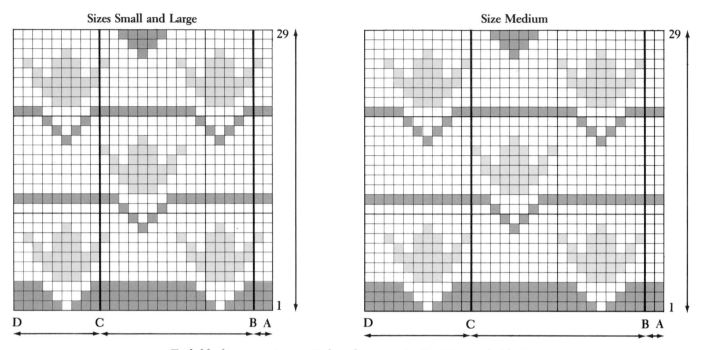

Sizes Small and Large   Size Medium

Each block represents one stitch and one row in Tunisian crochet knit
Work A to B one time, then B to C 4 (4, 5) times, then C to D one time

Row 1 of chart across next 75 (85, 91) sts as follows: A to B: With MC, k2; B to C: *With MC, k3 (4, 3); with A, k1; with MC, k12 (13, 12)*, repeat * to * 3 (3, 4) times more; C to D: With MC, k3 (4, 3); with A, k1; with MC k5 (6, 5)—**Row 1 of chart completed**—with MC, k10 (10, 12).

In the same manner, work Rows 2 and 3 of chart, **beginning and ending with MC k10 (10, 12).**

Shape Sleeves: At end of 2nd half of row, with MC, ch 40; draw up a lp through each new ch (in same manner as for foundation row); with MC, k10 (10, 12); work Row 4 of chart across next 75 (85, 91) sts; with MC, k10 (10, 12); with a separate strand of MC, ch 40; draw up a lp through each new ch—175 (185, 195) lps on hook.

Next Row: With MC, k50 (50, 52); work Row 5 of chart across next 75 (85, 91) sts; with MC, k50 (50, 52).

In the same manner, work Rows 6–29 of chart, **beginning and ending with MC k50 (50, 52).**

After chart is completed, with MC only, work even in knit stitch for 3 rows.

Neck Shaping: Knit across first 72 (77, 82) sts; leave remaining sts unworked.

Next Row: K68 (73, 78), insert hook through center of next 2 vertical lps **simultaneously** (as for k), yo, draw through both lps (k2 tog made, repeat this sequence each time instructions call for k2 tog or dec of 1), k2.

Next Row: Knit.

In the same manner, dec 1 st at neck edge next row and every other row 1 time.

Knit even on 69 (74, 79) sts until piece measures 22″ (22½″, 23″) from beginning.

End as follows: Leaving a sufficient length of yarn to secure later, cut yarn; draw yarn end through lp remaining on hook.

Leaving center 31 sts free, shape opposite side of neck edge to correspond.

BACK

With MC only, work as for front through sleeve shaping. Knit even on 175 (185, 195) sts until piece measures 20″ (20½″, 21″) from beginning.

Neck Shaping: Knit across first 71 (76, 81) sts; leave remaining sts unworked.

Working decreases in same manner as for front neckline, dec 1 st at neck edge next row and every other row 1 time.

Knit even on 69 (74, 79) sts until piece measures 22″ (22½″, 23″) from beginning.

Leaving center 33 sts free, shape opposite side of neck edge to correspond.

FINISHING

With right sides facing, using standard crochet hook and MC, join front to back at shoulder seams with sl st, matching stitches and inserting hook through centers of vertical lps (as for k) but from wrong side of work.

NOTE: Pick up stitches from an edge by inserting hook through center of vertical lp (as for k), yo, draw up a lp.

Neckband: With right side facing, MC and flexible afghan hook, begin at center back and pick up 112 (116, 120) lps evenly spaced around neck opening. Work off in usual manner.

Rib: **Rows 1–5:** K2, p1, *k3, p1*, repeat * to * around, ending with k1; end.

With right sides facing, standard crochet hook, MC and sl st, join short edges of neckband together.

Cuff: With right side facing, MC and H/14″ afghan hook, pick up 88 (92, 96) lps evenly spaced at sleeve edge. Work off in usual manner.

Rib: **Row 1:** K1, (k2 tog)—2 times, p1, *(k2 tog)—3 times, p1*, repeat * to * across; *Size Small Only:* End with (k2 tog)—2 times, k1—51 sts; *Size Medium Only:* End with (k2 tog)—2 times, k1, p1, k3—55 sts; *Size Large Only:* End with k3, p1, k2—58 sts.

All Sizes: **Rows 2–5:** *K3, p1*, repeat * to * across, ending with k3 (3, 2).

Repeat on other sleeve edge.

With right sides facing, standard crochet hook, MC and sl st, join sleeve and side seams.

Edging: With standard crochet hook and MC, begin at center back of neckband by inserting hook through center of vertical lp (as for k), yo, draw a lp through,*insert hook through center of vertical lp, yo, draw a lp through that lp **and** through lp on hook*, repeat * to * around.

End as follows: Leaving a sufficient length of yarn to secure later, cut yarn; insert hook into first st of edging rnd, yo, draw yarn end through to right side of work (weave back through to wrong side with tapestry needle before securing).

Work edging around cuffs and bottom rib in same manner.

Secure and trim loose ends.

Appliqué

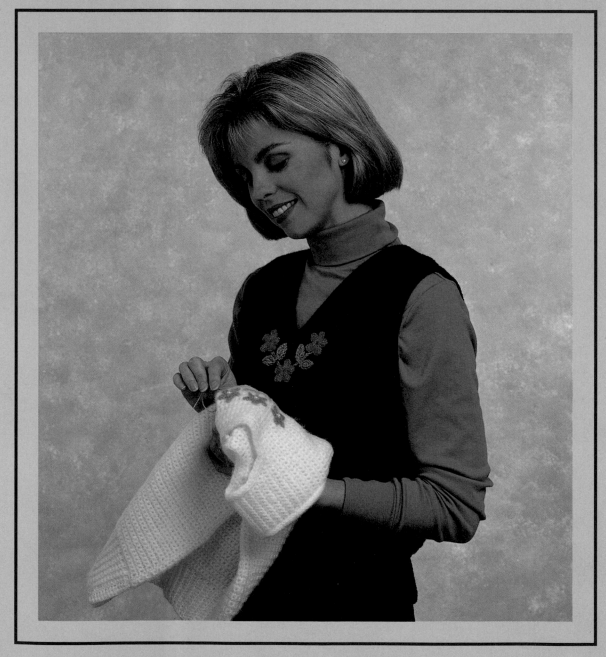

Two Flowered Pullovers

INTERMEDIATE

Appliquéd roses and violets lend romance
to these delightfully feminine sweaters.

SIZE

Small (Medium, Large)
Finished bust: 38″ (42″, 46″)
Back length: 21″ (21½″, 22″)

MATERIALS

Round-Neck with Violets

Brunswick Windmist (brushed, worsted weight Orlon acrylic), 1¾ oz/135 yd balls: 6 (6, 7) balls
Pale Yellow (MC)

Brunswick Sportmist (brushed, sport weight acrylic),
1¾ oz/175 yd balls: 1 ball each Lilac (A) and
Green (B)

Three 6mm craft pearls, cream-colored sewing
thread, sewing needle

V-Neck with Roses

Patons Super Wool (worsted weight, machine-
washable wool), 1¾ oz/116 yd balls: 7 (8, 9) balls
Black (MC)

Patons Pearl Twist (sport weight acrylic and nylon
blend), 1¾ oz/136 yd balls: 1 ball each Bright Pink
(A) and Bright Green (B)

Both Sweaters

Sizes E, I, and J crochet hooks (or size for gauge);
tapestry needle

GAUGE

15 sts = 4″; 18 rows = 4″ (in pattern st)
Check gauge to assure proper fit.

SEE

Decreasing/Single Crochet, Reverse Slip Stitch,
Surface Slip Stitch, and Working in the Round

Round-Neck with Violets

FRONT

Bottom Rib: With MC and I hook, ch 14.

Row 1: Sc in 2nd ch from hook and each ch across—
13 sts.

Rows 2–71 (79, 87): Ch 1, turn, sc in back lp only
of first st and each st across. Ch 1, work 71 (79, 87)
sc evenly spaced across long edge of rib. Change to J
hook.

Body: Row 1: Ch 1, turn, sc through both lps of first
st and each st across.

Repeat Row 1 until piece measures 13½″ from beginning; end.

Armhole Shaping: Sk first 10 (11, 12) sts, rejoin yarn
and sc across next 51 (57, 63) sts; leave remaining sts
unworked.

Continuing in sc, dec 1 st each edge next row and
every 3rd row 2 times.

Work even in sc on 45 (51, 57) sts until piece measures
18″ (18½″, 19″) from beginning.

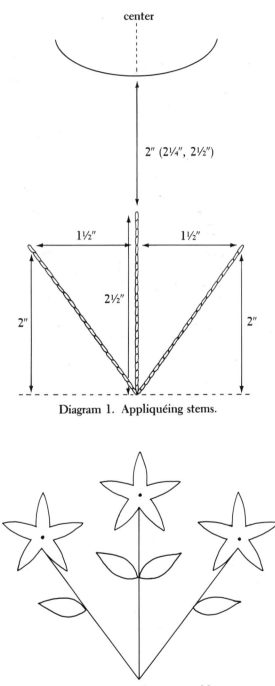

center

2" (2¼", 2½")

1½" 1½"

2½"

2" 2"

Diagram 1. Appliquéing stems.

Diagram 2. Appliqué assembly.

Neck Shaping: Sc across first 14 (16, 18) sts; leave remaining sts unworked.

Continuing in sc, dec 1 st at neck edge next row and every other row 2 times.

Work even in sc on 11 (13, 15) sts until piece measures 21" (21½", 22") from beginning.

Leaving center 17 (19, 21) sts free, shape opposite side of neck edge to correspond.

APPLIQUÉ

Violet (**make three**): With A and size E hook, ch 3, sl st in first ch to form ring. *Ch 4, sl st in 2nd ch from hook, sc in next ch, hdc in next ch, sl st into ring*, repeat * to * 4 times more; end.

Leaf (**make four**): With B and size E hook, ch 7. Sl st in 2nd ch from hook, *sc in next ch, hdc in next 2 ch, sc in next ch, sl st in last ch*; **working into other side of ch**, sl st in first ch and repeat * to * across; end.

Stem: With B and size E hook, ch 15 (should measure approximately 2½"); end. Being careful not to twist chain, pin chain to garment **as shown in Diagram 1.** Using B and tapestry needle, sew down with small running sts.

With B and size E hook, ch 29 (should measure approximately 4¾"). Pin chain to garment and sew down in same manner as for first chain.

Center a violet at each stem end **as shown in Diagram 2;** pin down. Using A and tapestry needle, sew down with small running sts along entire outer edge of violet.

Pin leaves to garment **as shown in Diagram 2.** Using B and tapestry needle, sew down in same manner as for violet.

Using sewing thread and sewing needle, sew a pearl at each flower center.

Round-Neck with Violets

V-Neck with Roses

V-Neck with Roses

FRONT

Work as for Round-Neck with Violets **to** armhole shaping.

Armhole/Neck Shaping: Sk first 10 (11, 12) sts, rejoin yarn and sc across next 25 (28, 31) sts; leave remaining sts unworked.

Continuing in sc, dec 1 st each edge next row and every 3rd row 2 times.

Work even in sc on 19 (22, 25) sts for 2 rows.

Continuing in sc, dec 1 st **at neck edge only** next row and every 3rd row 7 (8, 9) times.

Work even in sc on 11 (13, 15) sts for 2 rows.

Leaving center st free, shape opposite side to correspond.

APPLIQUÉ

Rose **(make three):** With A and size E hook, ch 4, sl st in first ch to form ring. *Ch 3, [(yo)—2 times, insert hook in ring, yo, draw up a lp, (yo, draw through 2 lps)—2 times], repeat [to] 1 time more, yo, draw through all 3 lps on hook, ch 4, sl st into ring*, repeat * to * 4 times more; end.

Leaf **(make four):** With B and size E hook, ch 7. Sl st in 2nd ch from hook, *sc in next ch, hdc in next 2 ch, sc in next ch, sl st in last ch*; **working into other**

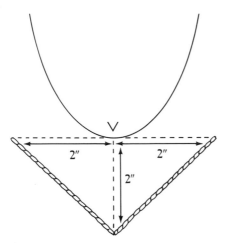

Diagram 3. Appliquéing stems.

Diagram 4. Appliqué assembly.

side of ch, sl st in first ch and repeat * to * across; end.

Stem: With B and size E hook, ch 29 (should measure approx 5¼″); end. Being careful not to twist chain, pin chain to garment **as shown in Diagram 3.** Using B and tapestry needle, sew down with small running sts.

Center a rose at each end and at V of stem **as shown in Diagram 4;** pin down. Using A and tapestry needle, sew down with small running sts along entire outer edge of rose.

Pin leaves to garment **as shown in Diagram 4.** Using B and tapestry needle, sew down in same manner as for rose.

BACK (both sweaters)

Work as for front until piece measures 13½″ from beginning; end.

Armhole Shaping: Sk first 10 (11, 12) sts, rejoin yarn and sc across next 51 (57, 63) sts; leave remaining sts unworked.

Continuing in sc, dec 1 st each edge next row and every 3rd row 2 times.

Work even in sc on 45 (51, 57) sts until piece measures 19½″ (20″, 20½″) from beginning.

Neck Shaping: Sc across first 14 (16, 18) sts; leave remaining sts unworked.

Continuing in sc, dec 1 st at neck edge every row 3 times.

Work even in sc on 11 (13, 15) sts for 2 rows.

Leaving center 17 (19, 21) sts free, shape opposite side of neck edge to correspond.

FINISHING (both sweaters)

With right sides facing, sew front to back at shoulder and side seams.

Edging: With right side facing, MC and I hook, start at center back and work 1 rnd sc around neck opening (**Note:** For V-neck work sc 3 tog at V); join with sl st to first sc.

Ch 1, don't turn, work 1 rnd reverse sl st into previous rnd; join with sl st to first reverse sl st.

Ch 1, don't turn, working **below** previous rnd, work 1 rnd surface sl st around posts of first edging rnd; join with sl st to first sl st.

Repeat the last rnd 1 time more; end.

Finish armhole edges in same manner.

Secure and trim loose ends.

Textured Pullover with Appliqué

INTERMEDIATE

*A garland of pastel roses adds folkloric charm
to this textured pullover.*

SIZE

Small (Medium, Large)
Finished bust: 38″ (42″, 46″)
Back length: 22″ (22½″, 23″)
Sleeve inseam: 19″ (19½″, 20″)

MATERIALS

Bernat Berella "4" (worsted weight acrylic), 3½ oz/
240 yd balls: 6 (7, 8) balls Cream (MC)
Bernat Berella Sportspun (sport weight acrylic),
1¾ oz/185 yd balls: 1 ball each Light Pink (A),
Bright Pink (B), and Green (C)
Sizes E, J, and K crochet hooks (or size for gauge);
tapestry needle
Five 6mm craft pearls, cream-colored sewing
thread, sewing needle

GAUGE

11 sts = 3″; 12 rows = 3″ (in pattern st)
Check gauge to assure proper fit.

SEE

Decreasing/Single Crochet, Increasing, Seed
Pattern, Surface Slip Stitch, and Working in the
Round

FRONT

Bottom Rib: With MC only and J hook, ch 14.

Row 1: Sc in 2nd ch from hook and each ch across—
13 sts.

Rows 2–69 (77, 85): Ch 1, turn, sc in back lp only
of first st and each st across. Ch 1, work 69 (77, 85)
sc evenly spaced across long edge of rib. Change to K
hook.

Body: Row 1 (wrong side): Ch 1, turn, sc in front lp
only of first st and each st across.

Row 2: Ch 1, turn, sc in both lps of first st, *sk next
st current row, dc in unused lp of sc 1 row below, sc
in both lps next st current row*, repeat * to * across.

Row 3: Repeat Row 1.

Row 4: Ch 1, turn, sk first st current row, dc in unused
lp of sc 1 row below, *sc in both lps next st current
row, sk next st current row, dc in unused lp of sc 1
row below*, repeat * to * across.

Repeat Rows 1–4, ending with Row 4, until piece
measures 14″ from beginning; end.

Armhole Shaping: Sk first 8 sts, rejoin yarn and work
Row 1 across next 53 (61, 69) sts; leave remaining sts
unworked.

Working even on 53 (61, 69) sts, repeat Rows 2–4 one
time; change to J hook.

Border: Ch 1, turn, sc in both lps of first st and each
st across.

Repeat the last row 11 times more (**border ends**);
change to K hook to resume pattern stitch.

Repeat Rows 3–4, then Rows 1–4 one time.

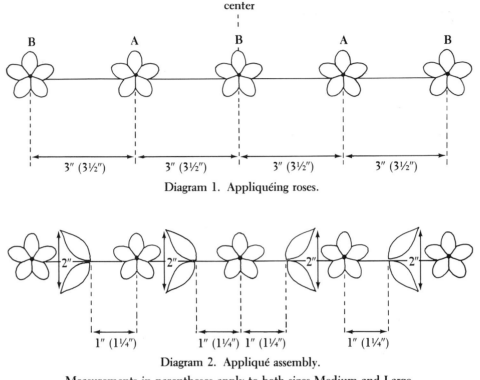

Diagram 1. Appliquéing roses.

Diagram 2. Appliqué assembly.

Measurements in parentheses apply to both sizes Medium and Large.

Neck Shaping: Work Row 1 across first 21 (25, 29) sts; leave remaining sts unworked.

Next (Dec) Row: Ch 1, turn, sk first st (**dec made**), sk next st current row, dc in unused lp of sc 1 row below, then complete as for Row 2 across.

Next (Dec) Row: Repeat Row 3, ending with sc 2 tog (**dec made**).

Next (Dec) Row: Ch 1, turn, sk first st (**dec made**), sc in both lps next st current row, then complete as for Row 4 across.

Next (Dec) Row: Repeat Row 1, ending with sc 2 tog (**dec made**).

Working even on 17 (21, 25) sts, repeat Rows 2–4, then Rows 1–4 one (one, two) times.

Size Medium Only: Repeat Rows 1–2 one time more.

All Sizes: Leaving center 11 sts free, shape opposite side of neck edge to correspond.

APPLIQUÉ

Rose (make two with A and three with B): With size E hook, ch 4, sl st in first ch to form ring. *Ch 3, [(yo)—2 times, insert hook in ring, yo, draw up a lp, (yo, draw through 2 lps)—2 times], repeat [to] 1 time more, yo, draw through all 3 lps on hook, ch 4, sl st into ring*, repeat * to * 4 times more; end.

Leaf (make eight): With C and size E hook, ch 7. Sl st in 2nd ch from hook, *sc in next ch, hdc in next 2 ch, sc in next ch, sl st in last ch*; **working into other side of ch,** sl st in first ch and repeat * to * across; end.

Stem: Stem is worked on border panel, between stitches, with surface slip stitch. Yarn is held at back of work throughout. It is important that stitch tension be neither too tight nor too loose, and that a sufficient length of yarn be left at **each** end to secure later.

With right side of front facing, C and size E hook, begin as follows: Count over 4 (4, 8) sts from **your** right, insert hook, **from front to back,** in space between 4th and 5th (4th and 5th, 8th and 9th) sts horizontally and **between** Rows 6 and 7 vertically. Holding yarn at back of work, yo, draw up a lp; *insert hook in sp directly beside sp just worked, yo, draw up a lp and draw that lp through the lp on hook*, repeat * to * across, leaving last 4 (4, 8) sts free.

Place roses **as shown in Diagram 1;** pin down. Using the corresponding yarn color and tapestry needle, sew down with small running stitches along entire outer edge of rose.

Pin leaves to garment **as shown in Diagram 2.** Sew down in same manner as for rose.

Using sewing thread and sewing needle, sew a pearl at each flower center.

BACK

Work as for front through armhole shaping.

Working even on 53 (61, 69) sts, repeat Rows 2–4, then Rows 1–4, ending with Row 4 (2, 4), until piece measures 20½″ (21″, 21½″) from beginning.

Neck Shaping: Work first neck shaping row of front.

Sizes Small and Large Only: Work decrease rows of front.

Size Medium Only: Next (Dec) Row: Ch 1, turn, sk first st (**dec made**), sc in both lps next st current row, then complete as for Row 4 across.

> Next (Dec) Row: Repeat Row 1, ending with sc 2 tog (**dec made**).

> Next (Dec) Row: Ch 1, turn, sk first st (**dec made**), sk next st current row, dc in unused lp of sc 1 row below, then complete as for Row 2 across.

> Next (Dec) Row: Repeat Row 3, ending with sc 2 tog (**dec made**).

All Sizes: Working even on 17 (21, 25) sts, repeat Row 2 (4, 2).

Leaving center 11 sts free, shape opposite side of neck edge to correspond.

SLEEVES (make two)

Work rib as for front but for 28 (30, 32) rows. Ch 1, work 31 (35, 39) sc evenly spaced across long edge of rib. Change to K hook.

Rows 1–4: Work Rows 1–4 of front on 31 (35, 39) sts.

Row 5 (Inc): Increasing 1 st each side, repeat Row 1.

Row 6: Repeat Row 4.

Rows 7–8: Repeat Rows 1–2.

Row 9 (Inc): Repeat Row 5.

Repeat Rows 2–9 six times more, then Rows 2–6 one time.

Working even on 61 (65, 69) sts, repeat Rows 1–4, ending with right side row, until piece measures 21″ (21½″, 22″) from beginning.

FINISHING

With right sides facing, sew front to back at shoulder seams, sleeves to sleeve openings, sleeve and side seams.

Neckband: With right side facing, MC and size J hook, start at center back and work 58 (62, 66) sc evenly spaced around neck opening; join with sl st to first sc; end.

Rib: With MC and J hook, ch 6.

Row 1: Sc in 2nd ch from hook and each ch across— 5 sts.

Rows 2–58 (62, 66): Ch 1 turn, sc in back lp only of first st and each st across. Ch 1, work 58 (62, 66) sc evenly spaced across long edge of rib.

Starting at center back, with right sides facing, sew neckband to neck opening and short edges of neckband together.

Secure and trim loose ends.

Crochet Stitches and Techniques

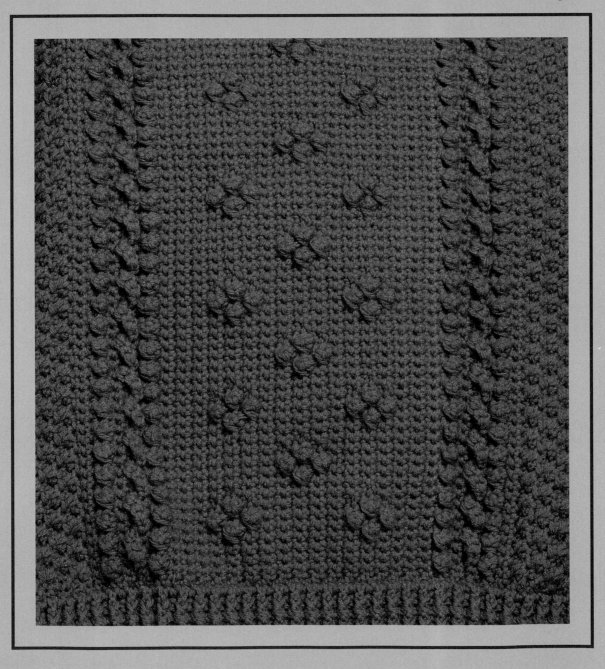

Basic Stitches and Techniques

HOLDING THE HOOK AND THE YARN

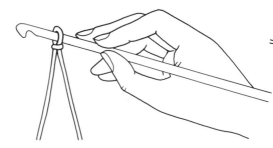 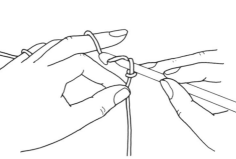 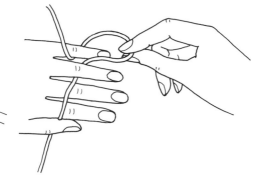

Hold the hook in your right hand, as you would a pencil.

Hold the yarn and the work in your left hand.

Stranding the yarn through the fingers of the left hand, as shown, helps maintain the slight tension necessary for the yarn to flow evenly and freely.

LEFT-HANDED CROCHET

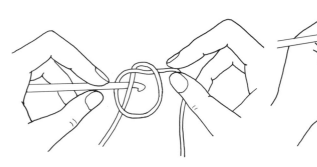

Hold the hook in your left hand.

Hold the yarn and the work in your right hand.

To see how to work a stitch left-handed, hold a mirror beside the illustration. The mirror will reverse the illustration and show how to work the stitch with your left hand.

BASE CHAIN (ch)

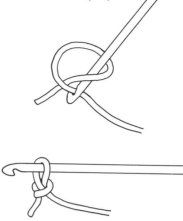

Crochet starts with a base chain. Begin by making a slip knot. Make a loop. Draw the yarn through the loop and tighten.

Wrap the yarn over the hook. Draw the yarn through the loop on the hook to form another loop.

Repeat as many times as required. The loop on the hook is **not** included in the number of chains specified in patterns.

SLIP STITCH (sl st)

Insert the hook into the 2nd chain from hook. Wrap the yarn over the hook. Draw the yarn through **both** the chain and the loop on the hook in one continuous motion—**slip stitch made.**

SINGLE CROCHET (sc)

Insert the hook into the 2nd chain from hook. Wrap the yarn over the hook. Draw the yarn through the chain.

Wrap the yarn over the hook again. Draw the yarn through both loops on the hook—**single crochet made.**

151

HALF DOUBLE CROCHET (hdc)

 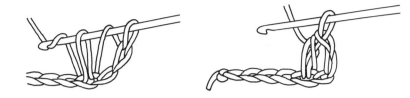

Wrap the yarn over the hook. Insert the hook into the 3rd chain from hook. Draw the yarn through the chain.

Wrap the yarn over the hook again. Draw the yarn through all 3 loops on the hook—**half double crochet made.**

DOUBLE CROCHET (dc)

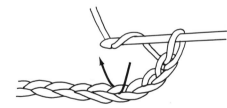 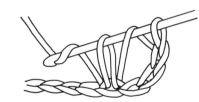

Wrap the yarn over the hook. Insert the hook into the 4th chain from hook. Draw the yarn through the chain.

Wrap the yarn over the hook again. Draw the yarn through the first 2 loops on the hook.

Wrap the yarn over the hook again. Draw the yarn through both loops remaining on the hook—**double crochet made.**

TRIPLE CROCHET (tr)

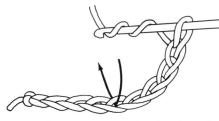  

Wrap the yarn over the hook twice. Insert the hook into the 5th chain from hook. Draw the yarn through the chain.

Wrap the yarn over the hook again. Draw the yarn through the first 2 loops on the hook.

Wrap the yarn over the hook again. Draw the yarn through the next 2 loops on the hook.

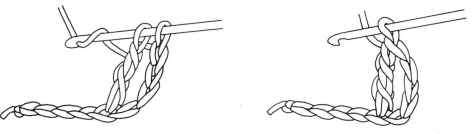

Wrap the yarn over the hook again. Draw the yarn through both loops remaining on the hook—**triple crochet made.**

WORKING IN ROUNDS

Make the required number of chains.

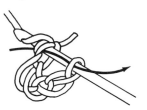 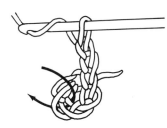

Join with a slip stitch to form a ring by inserting the hook into the first chain and drawing the yarn through both the chain and the loop on the hook.

Then, chain (as for the turning chain when working rows) and work subsequent stitches of the first round into the center of the ring.

WORKING IN ROWS

The first row is made by working across the base chain as described under basic stitches. Note that one or more chains were skipped at the beginning of the row. These skipped chains resemble the stitch being worked and often count as the first stitch. The number of chains skipped depends on the stitch being used: 1 for single crochet, 2 for half double crochet, 3 for double crochet, and 4 for triple crochet. The number of chains required for the base chain is always greater than the number of stitches in the first row.

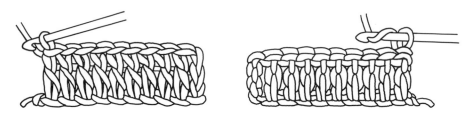

At the end of each row, the work must be turned before the next row can be worked. To turn, one or more chains must be made. The number of chains made depends on the stitch being used: 1 for single crochet, 2 for half double crochet, 3 for double crochet, and 4 for triple crochet.

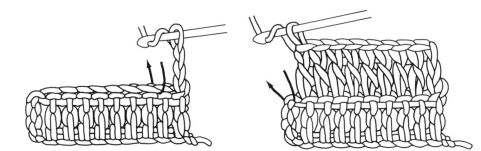

The turning chain often counts as the first stitch of the row. If so, skip the first stitch of the row and work a stitch into the turning chain of the last row when the end of row is reached.

If the turning chain does not count as the first stitch, don't skip the first stitch and don't work into the turning chain of the last row.

Unless otherwise specified, work into both loops at the top of each stitch of the last row.

DECREASING (dec)

Decreases are made by working two stitches together.

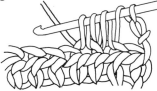
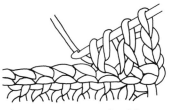

To decrease one single crochet within or at the end of a row: Insert the hook into the next stitch; wrap the yarn over the hook; draw a loop through. Repeat into the next stitch; there are 3 loops on the hook. Wrap the yarn over the hook again; draw through all 3 loops on the hook—**decrease made.**

To decrease one single crochet at the beginning of a row: Chain one, turn, skip the first stitch of the row. Don't work a stitch into the turning chain at the end of the **next** row.

To decrease one half double crochet within or at the end of a row: Wrap the yarn over the hook; insert the hook into the next stitch; wrap the yarn over the hook again; draw a loop through. Repeat into the next stitch; there are 5 loops on the hook. Wrap the yarn over the hook again; draw through all 5 loops on the hook—**decrease made.**

Work beginning of row decreases as for single crochet.

To decrease one double crochet within or at the end of a row: Wrap the yarn over the hook; insert the hook into the next stitch; wrap the yarn over the hook; draw a loop through; wrap the yarn over the hook again; draw through the first 2 loops on the hook. Repeat into the next stitch; there are 3 loops on the hook. Wrap the yarn over the hook again; draw through all 3 loops on the hook—**decrease made.**

To decrease one double crochet at the beginning of a row: Chain two, turn, skip the first stitch of the row. Don't work a stitch into the turning chain at the end of the **next** row.

INCREASING (inc)

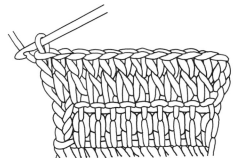

To increase one single, half double, double, or triple crochet (double shown), simply work two stitches into the same stitch.

JOINING NEW YARN

Always join new yarn at the end of a row. To join new yarn in single, half double, double, or triple crochet (double shown), work in the usual manner until 2 loops remain on the hook. Draw through both loops with the new yarn. Be sure to leave a sufficient length of yarn (approximately 4"), in both the old and the new yarn, to secure later.

ENDING

Work the last stitch in the usual manner. Cut the yarn, leaving a sufficient length to secure later (approximately 4"). Wrap the yarn end over the hook. Draw the yarn through the loop remaining on the hook, tightening gently.

CHANGING COLOR

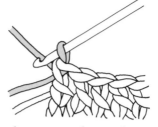

To change color in single, half double, double, or triple crochet (double shown), work in the usual manner until 2 loops remain on the hook. Draw through both loops on the hook with the new color.

When changing color at the end of a row, make the turning chain with the new color.

When changing color within a row, carry the color not in use loosely across the wrong side of the work, and work over it with the new color.

WORKING INTO ONE LOOP ONLY

Working into one loop only leaves the unused loop free, creating a ridge.

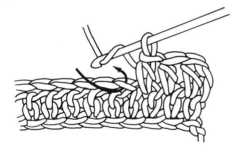

Working into the back loop only creates a ridge on the side of the fabric being worked. The fabric created when working in this manner is more elastic than most crochet stitches, and is frequently used for ribbing.

Working into the front loop only creates a ridge on the opposite side of the fabric.

WORKING AROUND POSTS

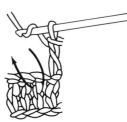

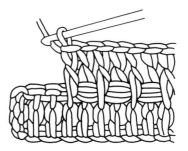

To work a double crochet around the post of a stitch from the **front**; known as a front post double crochet (**fpdc**): Wrap the yarn over the hook, insert the hook from **front to back** into the space between two stitches. Then, bring the hook to the front of the work again, through the space between the second of the stitches and the **next** stitch. Complete the stitch in the usual manner.

To work a double crochet around the post of a stitch from the **back**, known as a back post double crochet (**bpdc**): Wrap the yarn over the hook, insert the hook from **back to front** into the space between two stitches. Then, bring the hook to the back of the work again, through the space between the second of the stitches and the **next** stitch. Complete the stitch in the usual manner.

Double crochet rib is made by working front post and back post double crochets alternately across the row.

WORKING WITH CHAIN SPACES

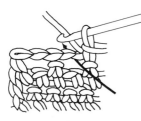

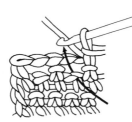

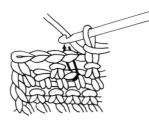

To work **in** a chain space: Insert the hook, from front to back, into the **space** below the chain. Complete the stitch in the usual manner.

To work **in front** of a chain space: Holding the chain to the **back** of the work, insert the hook, from front to back, into the **skipped stitch** of the **previous row**. Wrap the yarn over the hook; draw up a loop to the height of the current row. Complete the stitch in the usual manner.

To work **behind** a chain space: Holding the chain to the **front** of the work, insert the hook, from front to back, into the **skipped stitch** of the **previous row**. Wrap the yarn over the hook; draw up a loop to the height of the current row. Complete the stitch in the usual manner.

BUTTONHOLES

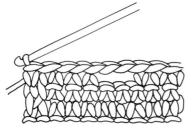

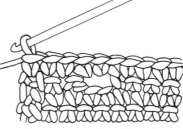

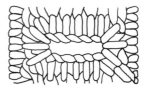

First Row: Work to the position of the buttonhole. Make the number of chains specified for the buttonhole. Skip the same number of stitches. Work into the next and subsequent stitches.

Second Row: Work to the chain space of the last row. Work one stitch into the chain space for each chain. Work into the next and subsequent stitches.

Reinforce crocheted buttonholes with buttonhole stitch, using a tapestry needle and matching yarn.

Special Stitches and Techniques

CLUSTERS
Clusters are made by working several double crochet stitches together (three shown).

Wrap the yarn over the hook; insert the hook into the chain; wrap the yarn over the hook; draw a loop through; wrap the yarn over the hook again; draw through the first 2 loops on the hook.

Repeat into the **same** chain two times more—there are 4 loops on the hook.

Wrap the yarn over the hook again; draw through all 4 loops on the hook—**cluster made.**

REVERSE SLIP STITCH

Reverse Slip Stitch is used for edging. It is worked from **left to right** into a base row of single crochet.

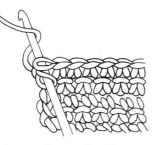

At the end of the single crochet base row, chain one, but **don't turn.** Keeping the yarn to the left of the work, insert the hook from **front to back** under both loops of the last stitch worked. Wrap the yarn over the hook in a **back to front** direction. Draw the yarn through **both** the stitch and the loop on the hook in one continuous motion.

Insert the hook under the next stitch to **your right.** Wrap the yarn and draw through in the same manner as for the first stitch.

SURFACE SLIP STITCH

Surface Slip Stitch is used to add color and/or texture to completed crocheted fabrics. The yarn is held at the back of the work throughout. It is important that the stitch tension be neither too tight nor too loose, and that a sufficient length of yarn be left at each end to secure later.

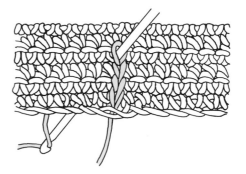

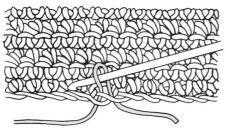

To work a vertical line, begin at the lower edge of the fabric by inserting the hook from **front to back** into the space **between** two stitches. Holding the yarn at the back of the work, wrap the yarn over the hook. Draw the yarn through to the front of the work.

Insert the hook from **front to back** into the space directly above the space just worked. Wrap the yarn over the hook and draw it through to the front of the work **and** through the loop on the hook in one continuous motion. Work subsequent stitches in the same manner.

To work a horizontal line, begin at the edge to your right and work in the same manner, around the posts of stitches, into the spaces between **rows.**

CHAIN BOBBLES

Chain Bobbles are made on wrong-side rows as follows:

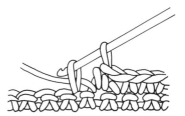

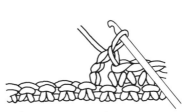

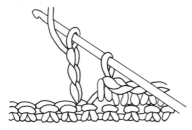

Single crochet in the stitch before the bobble. Insert the hook in the next stitch. Wrap the yarn over the hook. Draw a loop through.

Wrap the yarn over the hook. Draw a loop through to form a chain. Repeat two times more for a total of three chains.

Wrap the yarn over the hook again. Draw through both loops on the hook. Single crochet in the next stitch. This "crumples" the chain, forming a bobble on the right side of the work.

TRIPLE CROCHET BOBBLES

Triple Crochet Bobbles are made on wrong-side rows by working a slip stitch in the stitch before and in the stitch after a triple crochet. This "crumples" the triple crochet, forming a bobble on the right side of the work. These bobbles can be aligned or staggered for an entire fabric, used for a single row, or arranged in a pattern.

MOSS PATTERN

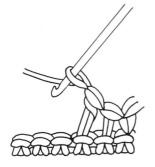

Moss Pattern is made on wrong-side rows by working a slip stitch in the stitch before and in the stitch after a half double crochet. This "crumples" the half double crochet, forming a texture pattern on the right side of the work.

SPIKE STITCH

Spike Stitches are made by working into a previous row.

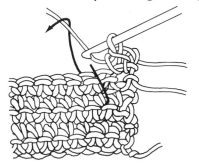

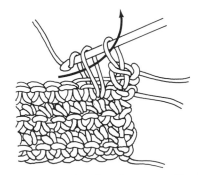

Insert the hook, from front to back, into the space below the stitch (into the same place that stitch was worked). Wrap the yarn over the hook. Draw up a loop to the height of the current row.

Wrap the yarn over the hook again. Draw through both loops on the hook.

CABLES

Cables are worked on right-side rows. Begin by working a single crochet in the stitch before the first cable.
Chain three, skip the next two stitches, single crochet in the next stitch, **turn** the work.

Single crochet in each of the three chains just completed.

Slip stitch in the next stitch, **turn** the work.

Working **behind** the cable just completed, work one single crochet in the first of the skipped stitches, then two single crochets in the second of the skipped stitches.

    Repeat from the chain three across the work. End with a single crochet in the last stitch.

SEED PATTERN

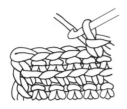

Begin by working a row of front loop only single crochet across the wrong side of the fabric. The unused (back) loops are free and form a ridge on the right side of the work.

On the next (right-side) row, work a single crochet into both loops of the first stitch. Skip the next stitch of the current row and work a double crochet into the unused loop of the single crochet one row below.

Work a single crochet into both loops of the next stitch of the current row. Repeat the last two stitches alternately across the fabric.

Repeat the first wrong-side row. Work the next right-side row in the same manner as the last right-side row, but begin with a double crochet (rather than a single crochet), to stagger the pattern.

Double Seed Pattern is made by alternately working **pairs** of single and double crochet, in the same manner, across the fabric.

STAR STITCH

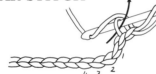

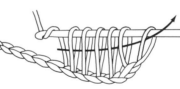

First Stitch: Insert the hook into the 2nd chain from hook. Wrap the yarn over the hook. Draw a loop through the chain. Repeat into the next 4 chains; there are 6 loops on the hook.

Wrap the yarn over the hook again. Draw through all 6 loops on the hook.

Wrap the yarn over the hook again. Draw through the loop on the hook (chain one made).

Second and Subsequent Stitches: Insert the hook under the chain one just made. Wrap the yarn over the hook. Draw up a loop. Insert the hook under both strands of the last loop of the last star made. Wrap the yarn over the hook. Draw up a loop. Insert the hook into the same chain used for the last loop of the last star. Wrap the yarn over the hook. Draw up a loop. Insert the hook into the next chain. Wrap the yarn over the hook. Draw up a loop. Repeat into the next chain; there are 6 loops on the hook.

Wrap the yarn over the hook again. Draw through all 6 loops on the hook. Chain one.

Finishing

Use as much care to finish a project as you do to crochet it and you'll be sure to have a garment you're proud to wear!

SECURING LOOSE ENDS

Thread the loose end through a tapestry needle. Weave the end through several stitches on the wrong side of the fabric, working several back stitches as you go to secure it. Don't work too tightly or go through to the right side of the work. Until you feel comfortable with this technique, it's helpful to check the right side of the fabric to make sure that it's still attractive before trimming the end.

BLOCKING

Blocking is seldom necessary since crochet produces a firm fabric. However, if blocking is required, begin by checking the yarn label. If the label says do not iron, or shows the symbol of an iron with an X through it, **don't** use an iron on the fabric; it could **melt**! Wet blocking must be done.

If the yarn label indicates that ironing is permitted, pin the garment piece to the desired shape on a padded surface (such as a thick bath towel). Then, cover the fabric with a pressing cloth and apply a **cool** iron **lightly** so as not to flatten the stitches. Let the piece cool before removing it.

To wet-block, pin the piece (with **rustproof** pins) to the desired shape on a padded surface. Cover with a damp cloth and leave in place until completely dry.

SEAMS

Begin by pinning the edges of the pieces together, with right sides facing, matching stitches and/or rows. Be particularly careful with stripes.

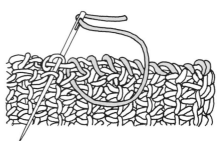

Overcast

This seaming method yields a flat, invisible seam and gives the garment a professional finish. Thread a tapestry needle with a length of yarn. Sew the pieces together by inserting the needle under one strand of yarn at the first edge, then over to and under one strand of yarn at the second edge.

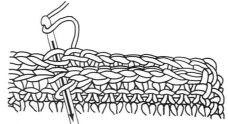

Slip Stitch

Use a crochet hook several sizes smaller than the one used to make the fabric and work loosely. Insert the hook through both pieces of fabric. Wrap the yarn over the hook and draw a loop through. Insert the hook through both pieces of fabric again; wrap the yarn over the hook and draw the yarn through both the fabric and the loop on the hook. Repeat the last step across the fabric.

EDGING

Crocheted garments usually require some type of crocheted-edge finishing. To make an attractive edge, stitches must be evenly spaced. There should be sufficient stitches for the edge not to pucker, but not so many that it curls. When a pattern calls for a certain number of stitches to be worked along an edge, this is the number of stitches that will yield an attractive edge.

Tunisian Crochet

Tunisian crochet is done with a special hook, known as an afghan hook. Afghan hooks are longer than conventional crochet hooks, of a uniform thickness, and have a knob at the end.

The most commonly used Tunisian crochet stitch is the basic afghan stitch. Less frequently seen are the Tunisian crochet knit and purl stitches, which resemble their knitting equivalents.

A Tunisian crochet fabric is thicker and less elastic than a knit fabric. Using lightweight yarn and a large hook minimizes the difference.

In Tunisian crochet, each row is composed of two halves—a "forward" or first half, worked from left to right, where loops are picked up and kept on the hook; and a "return" or second half, worked from right to left, where the loops are bound off. The last stitch of the return (second half) row always counts as the first stitch of the **next** forward (first half) row. The work is not turned, and the right side of the fabric is facing the crocheter at all times.

Tunisian crochet always begins with a foundation row.

FOUNDATION ROW

First half: Make the required number of chains. Insert the hook in the 2nd chain from hook. Wrap the yarn over the hook; draw a loop through the chain.

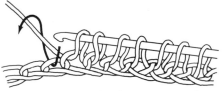

Repeat into each chain across, **keeping all of the loops on the hook.**

Second half: Wrap the yarn over the hook; draw the yarn through the first loop on the hook.

Wrap the yarn over the hook; draw the yarn through the next two loops on the hook. Repeat across until one loop remains on the hook—**foundation row complete.**

JOINING NEW YARN

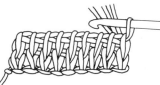

Always join new yarn at the end of the second half of a row. To join new yarn, work the second half of the row in the usual manner until two loops remain on the hook. Draw through both loops with the new yarn. Be sure to leave a sufficient length of yarn (approximately 4"), in both the old and the new yarn, to secure later.

PURL STITCH (p)

Work a foundation row.

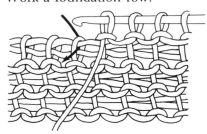

First half: Holding the yarn in front of the work, skip the first vertical loop below, insert the hook from **back to front** through the center of the next vertical loop (the hook should pass under the chain formed by the second half of the previous row). Wrap the yarn over the hook; draw a loop through. Repeat into each loop across, **keeping all the loops on the hook.**

Second half: Work as for the foundation row.

KNIT STITCH (k)

Work a foundation row.

First half: Holding the yarn in back of the work, skip the first vertical loop below, insert the hook from **front to back** through the center of the next vertical loop (the hook should pass under the chain formed by the second half of the previous row). Wrap the yarn over the hook; draw a loop through.

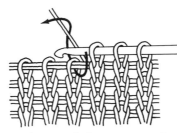

Repeat into each loop across, **keeping all the loops on the hook.**

Second half: Work as for the foundation row.

INCREASING (inc)

Increases are made in the first half of a row. Work to where an increase is indicated in the usual manner.

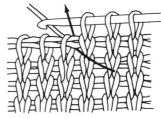

Insert the hook from **front to back** into the space **between** the stitch just worked and the next stitch (the hook should pass under the chain formed by the second half of the previous row). Wrap the yarn over the hook. Draw up a loop—**increase made.**

Work the next stitch and complete the row in the usual manner.

DECREASING (dec)

Decreases are made in the first half of a row. Work to where a decrease is indicated in the usual manner.

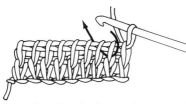

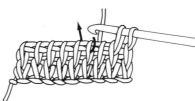

Insert the hook from **front to back** through the center of the **next two** vertical loops **simultaneously** (as for a knit stitch). Wrap the yarn over the hook. Draw the yarn through **both** of the loops—**decrease made.**

Work the next stitch and complete the row in the usual manner.

ENDING

Work the last stitch of the second half of a row in the usual manner. Cut the yarn, leaving a sufficient length to secure later (approximately 4″). Wrap the yarn end over the hook. Draw the yarn through the loop remaining on the hook, tightening gently.

CHANGING COLOR
End of Row

Work the second half of the last row of a color in the usual manner, until two loops remain on the hook. Drop the old color to the back of the work. Draw through both loops on the hook with the new color.

Within a Row

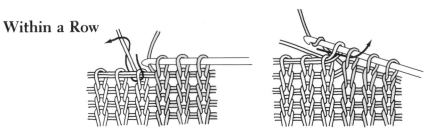

First Half: Change color on the stitch indicated by the pattern by drawing up a loop with the new color.

When working individual color motifs, wind a separate bobbin of yarn for each color section. Don't carry colors not in use. Simply drop colors not in use to the back of the work; they will then be in the proper place for the second half of the row.

A color not in use can be carried for a **few** stitches by stranding it **loosely** across the back of the work.

Second Half: Draw through each loop with the corresponding color, changing when the first loop of the new color is reached. Drop colors and carry in the same manner as for the first half of the row.

BOBBLES Bobbles are made in the first half of a row. Work to where a bobble is indicated in the usual manner.

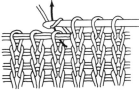

Wrap the yarn over the hook; insert the hook from **front to back** through the center of the next vertical loop (as for a knit stitch); wrap the yarn over the hook; draw a loop through.

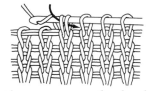

Wrap the yarn over the hook again; draw the yarn through the first two loops on the hook.

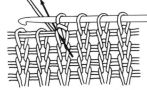

Repeat into the **same** stitch three times more.

Wrap the yarn over the hook again; draw the yarn through the first four loops on the hook.

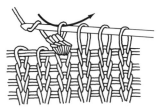

Wrap the yarn over the hook again; draw the yarn through the first loop on the hook—**bobble is complete.** Complete the row in the usual manner.

Index

Yarn Suppliers

For information about retail and mail order availability of the yarns featured in this book, contact:

Bernat Yarn & Craft Corp.
P.O. Box 387
Uxbridge, MA 01569

Berroco, Inc.
P.O. Box 367
Uxbridge, MA 01569

Brunswick Yarns
P.O. Box 276
Pickens, SC 29671

Classic Elite Yarns, Inc.
12 Perkins St.
Lowell, MA 01854

Patons Yarns
c/o Susan Bates, Inc.
212 Middlesex Ave.
Chester, CT 06412

Phildar USA
6110 Northbelt Pkwy.
Norcross, GA 30071

Pingouin Yarns
c/o Laninter Corp.
P.O. Box 1542
Mt. Pleasant, SC 29465

William Unger & Co.
P.O. Box 350
Willimantic, CT 06226

Reynolds Yarns
c/o JCA, Inc.
P.O. Box 158
West Townsend, MA 01474

The author would like to thank the yarn suppliers who kindly donated yarn for many of the projects included in this book.

All of us at Meredith® Press are dedicated to offering you, our customer, the best books we can create. We are particularly concerned that all of the instructions for making the projects are clear and accurate. We welcome your comments and would like to hear any suggestions you may have. Please address your correspondence to Customer Service Department, Meredith® Press, Meredith Corporation, 150 East 52 Street, New York, NY 10022.